Alfred Wong Partnership

Alfred Wong Partnership
Innovation and Knowledge

Texts by
Paolo Righetti

l'ARCAEDIZIONI

Photographic Credits
Albert Lam Beng Choon-AL Studio Life
(STB HQ Building and Robinson Point)
Hans Schlupp Photography (Raffles Marina)
Images-Tim Griffith courtesy of
"Architecture Now 1- A Visual from the
World's Premier Architects", publisher 1993-
Sigma Union Inc. (Odeon Towers).
All other images by Alfred Wong Partnership

Alfred Wong Partnership acknowledges
the valuable assistance of Angelo Vozzi
in this monograph.

Editorial Director USA
Pierantonio Giacoppo

Chief Editor of Collection
Maurizio Vitta

Publishing Coordinator
Franca Rottola

Graphic Design
ST Graphic

Editing
Martyn J. Anderson

Colour-separation
Litofilms Italia, Bergamo

Printing
Poligrafiche Bolis, Bergamo

First published April 1999

Copyright 1999
by l'Arca Edizioni

ISBN 88-7838-061-X

Contents

WITHDRAWN

Preface

by Alfred Wong Partnership

In the brief period of forty years, Alfred Wong Partnership's contribution to the cityscape of Singapore has been significant and diverse, producing comprehensive architecture on the cutting edge of design innovation and technology. The firm was founded by Alfred Wong in 1957, established during the post-war era, which heralded a new generation of architects who became the forerunners of present day Singapore. Since then, the last four decades witnessed Singapore undergoing vigorous changes on a massive social and economic scale. The infrastructure of the city and the built environment in particular, was to transform dramatically and many of Alfred Wong Partnership's buildings became an inextricable part of this 'upgrading', contributing significantly to the historic works of the Republic and its People. As a result, the company has a diverse range of award winning projects to its credit, that demonstrate considerable flexibility, with proven experience and qualified expertise in a number of specialised areas.

In 1968 a prominent contribution to Singapore's urbanscape was the Republic's first purpose built hotel, the Omni Marco Polo Hotel. Alfred Wong displayed extraordinary foresight in convincing the developers to build the only luxury hotel of international standard in Singapore. The result was an award winning design, having set a precedent as a forerunner in the initial phases of development in Singapore's Tourism Industry. Originally named Hotel Malaysia, the hotel was designed as two parallel curved blocks to accommodate three hundred guestrooms. An extension to the hotel in 1980 provided a further three hundred and eight rooms and a full services upgrade. This proved to be an intelligent and lucrative decision for both new owners and Alfred Wong Partnership alike, culminating in the 1983 Singapore Institute of Architects Award for Design Merit, and it was ranked as the fourth Best Hotel in the World by British Magazine 'Executive Travel'. This exemplary building demonstrates Alfred Wong Partnership's ability to successfully

Mr Alfred Wong's own house in Bin Tong Park.

perform an appropriate function for both investors and end users over a tested continuum of time.

Their earlier works also impacted on the residential sector, in particular, with the design of Mr Alfred Wong's own house. It is set amongst the intoxicatingly lush gardens of Bin Tong Park. Horizontal concrete planes float above the treetops, with a disciplined and restrained classicism contrasting with its natural parkland setting. It stands as a brilliantly executed homage to the modernist era. Alfred Wong Partnership has since continued to produce such innovative architecture and constantly broadened its portfolio in the last four decades, reflecting the rapid development of Singapore into an international, commercial city.

The company has made some valuable contributions to the educational sector, revealing a unique conglomeration of influences deriving from Catholicism, Modernism, and the Singaporean identification with the desire to produce architecture with a sense of responsibility. The Singapore Polytechnic of Technology is one of the country's leading higher education centres. The design is based on intelligent planning and environmentally passive design. The site plan configuration is in the form of parallel blocks, strategically placed in order to achieve consistent natural ventilation throughout all the teaching areas. An innovative windscoop device, designed with the aid of a wind tunnel, provides cross-ventilation to the massive workshop

blocks. By connecting each building to a system of walkways, a fluid pedestrian access is provided, creating quadrangles of open spaces in between, interfacing one group of buildings with another. The design was nationally recognised by The Singapore Institute of Architects Award for Design Merit in 1983. Such examples of innovative, exemplary thinking were epitomised in Prototype Primary and Secondary School designs successfully submitted by Alfred Wong Partnership to the Public Works Department in 1981. Deliberately designed to contrast against the regularity of the HDB block, the pitched roof line allows a non-horizontal massing to prevent the heaviness that is normally produced with long, four storey high buildings. The new design's purpose was to add variety to the standard designs then used by the Public Works Department and to facilitate any adaptations to the multitude of site conditions that may be encountered.

Today the work of the Partnership has identified with select building types for which it is specifically equipped to carry out research and design. Large scale buildings, in particular, have been focused upon its agenda for which the firm is well equipped to undertake research and conceptual development. These areas currently include buildings for: Higher Education Institutions and Facilities; Condominium and High Density Housing Schemes; Central Business Area and Urban Redevelopment of Commercial and Retail buildings; Recreational, Marina and Club Facilities;

Industrial and Warehouse Facilities; Ecclesiastical Buildings, Medical Buildings and Ancillary Facilities; Environmental and Landscape Design; Hotel and Tourist; Development Schemes; Master Planning.

The firm's comprehensive and holistic approach to design was nationally recognised in 1985, when Alfred Wong Partnership was nominated by the Singapore Institute of Architects to represent Singapore for the Robert Mathew Award. This comprised of entrants from all the Commonwealth countries, selected for their innovative contributions to architecture. By 1988, Alfred Wong Partnership's accomplishments had achieved international acclaim, in their nomination at the Belgrade Triennial of World Architecture as one of the 'Fifty Outstanding Architects of the World'.

Building on this extensive involvement with projects in Singapore, Alfred Wong Partnership diverged to extend its horizons and further develop skills in new environments abroad. In recognising the importance in the transfer of technology applicable in the case of specific projects and situations, the Partnership has successfully collaborated with several international firms. With a type of blending cultural osmosis occurring, a veritable source of information becomes available, with much to be gained by learning from each other's different cultures and value systems. The resulting interaction and global communication provides an impressive regional distribution of professional expertise and design innovation.

Alfred Wong Partnership has been associated with Peddle Thorp Architects since 1972. The association was formed to serve international clientele as well as local clients with overseas investments. (Since 1991 Alfred Wong Partnership has acquired shares from the Sydney Partnership whilst still maintaining a link with the Australian offices.) More recently the company has worked in collaboration with HOK International (Asia/Pacific) Limited and Wimberly Allison Tong and Goo (Hawaii). To broaden their scope of works, an Architectural Design Consultancy Service is provided, having completed Keppel Distripark for the PSA, Singapore and the Sukhumvit Road Service Apartments, Bangkok, Thailand.

The firm has also been called upon to export their skills to projects in Vietnam and the Peoples' Republic of China. The early nineties witnessed China plunged into a frenzy of capitalism. Foreign investment exploded by six hundred percent with many astute Singaporeans amongst the flood of investors. Alfred Wong Partnership completed their first major Chinese project in 1992, Holiday Inn Crowne Plaza, a five star international hotel built in Xiamen, a lucrative seaport opposite Taiwan. Since then, the firm has ventured onto their second major development in China. The UOB building, recently completed in 1996, is designed specifically for foreign business people, and is located in a district

hailed as Xiamen's equivalent of Wall Street.

The firm believes that Architects practising in newly developing countries carry a special responsibility in that investments in each new project represent a major expenditure within the framework of a developing economy. Accordingly, such fiscal expenditure should be made use of effectively and with flair and imagination. In recognising that each building does not exist in isolation but forms part of an urban landscape, the design input for each project in each location is differentiated so that they relate to their immediate environment, which is unique and distinct in itself. With this approach the firm has acquired an impressive list of local and international clients, many of whom have returned to commission the firm's services again. Alfred Wong Partnership's current international portfolio includes projects in Vietnam, Indonesia, Taiwan, Malaysia and China.

In 1994, Alfred Wong Partnership had developed to a point when conversion to a limited company became essential in order to broaden the scope of their services and upgrade the level of their contributions in a diverse range of projects both in Singapore and overseas. Involvement in diverse building types has kept them poised on the leading edge of contemporary design concepts and building technology providing a broad and stable base for the company. Their belief that each building design derives from the relevancy of specific

functional requirements and its environmental context duly accounts for their success in the honesty and diversity of their building designs.

A total of eight directors, including four directors who represent the younger group of architects, now form an intrinsic element in the organisation's visionary leadership of the company. While each of the partners has his own specialised area of expertise, a collaborative effort is invested into the decision-making and design of each project. This pooling of professional knowledge and experience, and the capacity to be involved from the earliest conceptual stage through to post-occupancy services after completion, is an indication of the firm's commitment to ensure each design's imminent success. Of fundamental importance is the close working relationship with each Client, propagating extensive productive discussions with a mutual exchange of ideas that lead to more qualified and sensitive design solutions. Their commitment to quality is certified by ISO 9001 standard, successfully attained in 1997.

Hence over the last forty years Alfred Wong Partnership has successfully balanced the inspirations of fresh, innovative ideas, together with a proven resource of an experienced professional body of knowledge. These basic philosophies have rocketed them to the leading edge of 'intelligent' building design. The challenge now is to continue build upon these four decades of achievement in the dedicated pursuit of architectural excellence.

Between Regionalism and the International Idiom

by Paolo Righetti

There are two recognizable sides to Alfred Wong's architecture: one is its regionalist connotations, the other its inclination towards the international idiom. Let us say at once that the one that appears to be prevalent is the international aspect of his approach. A quick and comprehensive survey of Wong's work reveals a picture of buildings which, though prevalently situated in Singapore, potentially belong to world architecture. In fact, though linked to a place through the specific nature of the site, these structures are projected by their idiom into an international dimension. It is only by looking under their surfaces that the other aspect can really be seen: that of its close, profound, and therefore non-obtrusive relationship with regionalism.

Moreover, the division and overlapping of local and external realities are generally characteristic of the history of Singapore, which is "contested", among others, by England, Japan (which occupied the city during World War II, from '42 to '45), the Commonwealth, and Malaysia until it attained its present status as an independent republic in 1965.

An international dimension which has passed through here, contributing, apart from its negative aspects and the conflict, to an enrichment which is always caused by trade and by the overlapping of different cultures.

In its materials, in the study of its components, in its constructional solutions, and in its distributional choices, the counterpoint between local tradition and international vocation therefore becomes a theme in a theme, a sophisticated game but never a matter of chance, a sort of "signature" of Wong's architecture. An element, this, that even runs through his horizontal architecture, in which the counterpoint is sometimes between different works. For example, the response to the sober solutions and "technological" morphology of the Nordic Centre, a complex destined for the enterprises of Scandinavian countries active in Singapore, is the strong connection, demanded by the client, with traditional identity, which is translated into the phytomorphism of the columns of the Tourist Promotion Board, a building in which the State is represented and which interfaces with the rest of the world.

This approach forms part of the more complex theme of how the world sees this geographical reality and how Singapore itself, knowing this, steps forward and intervenes, in a sort of short circuit, in order to present an image of itself, transforming some occasions, among which architecture itself, into vehicles of communication. What is involved here is the whole range of socio-cultural, economic, and political relationships. It is as if in some sort of "self-analysis" the mask were stripped off a certain way of presenting itself adopted by an enclave called on, after years of cultural and political dependence, to assume an independent and direct relationship with the rest of the world. Substantially, it is an occasion to choose what forms to give and what visibility to attribute to the substance of administrative and decisional choices. And it is certainly no news that it is architecture itself which is the first and easiest instrument for composing this system of enunciations. When this picture gets to the architect, it is already strongly delineated, because it is in the phase just before the project - the phase when choices are made regarding the functions, destinations, importance in terms of dimensions, and the posting of operations - that political control and economic power play their cards. As always, in this sense the architect is the instrument of the power that he represents. The architect doing this work can consider himself lucky if his professional activity happens to coincide with a positive historical moment, and we may be sure that substantially Wong's professional career intersected a very positive phase in the life of Singapore. Many of the works that he was commissioned fit perfectly into this picture, especially as vehicles of competition with the spread of an international attitude characterized by two recognizable elements, in which the most powerful forces are represented: the emergence of the dimensional factor and structuring in terms of the marketing of an expressive idiom.

The relationship with function and with the surroundings

The more than 40 years of activity of the Alfred Wong Partnership began in the lively postwar period, when important social and economic changes were taking place, and when, consequently, there was a need for a great many infrastructural works or, in any case, works of collective

interest. On becoming part of this mechanism, Wong's planning activities were immediately characterized by the importance and variety of the worked carried out. Starting with his first important work, the Omni Marco Polo Hotel, which was the first large international Hotel structure in Singapore and was built in two phases, the first of which in 1968 and, more recently, a sort of double completed in 1974. Then came the large complexes dedicated to learning, among which St.Joseph's Institution and the prestigious Polytechnic, completed in 1979. Connected, instead, with the world of production are the pharmaceutical complex built for Schering, which is a recent work, a few infrastructural works such as the Keppel Distripark, a big centre for the stocking and distribution of goods, a work commissioned by the port of Singapore, or the Nordic Centre, designed for research and development, but also to house a sort of "industrial incubator" for firms as yet unable to find a site of their own. Wong's exploration of the possibilities of tall buildings is carried out in different and mostly recent creations, among which the Odeon Tower, the complex for the Singapore Tourist Promotion Board, respectively of `92 and `95, the Robinson Point, and the Chinese Chamber of Commerce, with thirty floors at a height of 140 metres, a building still unfinished.

The theme of dimensions is central to Wong's work. The type of destinations chosen, the particular socio-economic context we referred to earlier, and the need to carry out

a representational function, which was often required in the works he was commissioned, found their first, almost obligatory synthesis in the dimensions of the works executed, a synthesis exactly expressed in terms of cubic metres and overall volume. Complexes like the Singapore Polytechnic are operations which, if only for their sheer size, are capable of bestowing a greater "weight" on a city, and of influencing its barycentres, with side-effects, of course, on the infrastructural, social, and economic aspects of the territory as a whole. With the imposing weight of such signs, one inevitably looks back on the historical stages of architecture characterized by exactly this dimensional factor, stages that have intersected the work of ordinary professionals but also the great masters. We are thinking of how much of Le Corbusier's work is characterized by just this aspect. Ranging from the dream of a city condensed into huge tenement blocks of great density, in order to free the territory (in Corbu's Unité d'habitation), to the structures for Chandigarh. Just as happened in the cases of the huge working-class residential complexes from the functionalist period down to the seventies, with any number of examples, beginning with the Hofe of Ehn. In some respects it calls to mind, even though it is an expression on quite a different scale, the imposing dimensional and idiomatic effect of the Mel'nikov. Or the soaring skyscrapers of the New York and Chicago schools. These infinite numbers of examples are all characterized by at least one common aspect, which holds also for Wong's architecture: the fact that they become signs, and manage to attract resources, destinies, and expectations. And to intervene in the evolution of an urban reality or a geographical context irreversibly, inextricably binding their names and their work to it.

Wong is currently at work all around Singapore, collaborating on projects in Malaysia, Vietnam and South China.

The heterogeneous nature of their ultimate use and the different contexts in which the works are localized, have produced another of the most important characteristics of Wong's architecture: a marked and perceptible difference in the kinds of project. This characteristic, though in itself neutral, is transformed into a positive value in acknowledging their methodological motivations and their approach: to avoid preconstituted forms and to derive one's choice from a study of the surrounding territory on which the work is to be built (resisting, however, the temptation to adopt a gratuitously local idiom) and crossing these elements with the relationships between functional values, and the compositional and spatial solutions of the materials.

The strong relationship with the terrain and its orography that characterizes the St. Joseph's Institution complex is an example. As is the symbolic correspondence between the highly technologized content of the Keppel Distripark and the idiom employed for its architecture: pilework dwellings suspended above ground level

(reserved for vehicular traffic), structures in which the constructive solutions, such as the network of tie beams, are visible and undisguised. The same international character of Wong's works is not the product of a choice of idiom, but the consequence of the representational dimension required by such operations as the construction of large international hotels, university centres designed for the global village and multinational companies in the industrial sector. Worlds which in architecture seem to enjoy some sort of extraterritorial status.

It is in this logical framework that one should interpret the dialogue with contemporaries that has characterized Wong's work, even in the past. In the course of his professional career seen in an historical perspective one finds references and quotations that emphasize, if there were any need to, the attention and effort that Wong dedicated to projects which were never fortuitous. The works he designed in the seventies, like Singapore Polytechnic are now part of an international triangulation involving the work of masters of architecture of quite different geographical-territorial extraction from across Europe, the Americas and the Orient. The use of a highly stylistic idiom of "notable" expressive force or the attempt to inject a sense of rhythm and order into the overall architectural design make Wong's work unique of its kind on the international scene, providing a yardstick for many other people's work.

Parallelisms and affinities do not derive only from the homogeneity

of research programmes and approaches common to many studios and architects situated in different parts of the world. At a certain point in this century a sort of international matrix began to characterise architecture, influencing the continuity of distinct historical and evolutional paths. Paths sometimes thousands of years old, in which a complex system of relationships between tradition and progress had gradually intertwined in ideal linear discourses that stood out for the identity of the cultural and traditional type they designated. The anti-historical approach of the modern movement and the experience of the International Style, unquestionably led to a fracture and a discontinuity in these evolutionary courses, while making, however, an important contribution in terms of provocation and methodological stimulus. This lack of continuity in motivations of a methodological character occasionally overlapped with the progressive affirmation of the international matrix. Forms, dimensions, recognizable and visible characteristics, a scale of values and of significance attributed to different functions, have increasingly been derived from models of living or from behavioural habits characteristic, for example, of Western realities and, therefore, distant from historically different social philosophies like those of the Orient and, to some extent, even those of Europe. Buildings to be consumed like objects, governed by the laws of the market and certainly badly matched with the approaches to living found in these other places.

Fortunately, there has been a sort of spontaneous emergence of many pockets of cultural resistance. The stylistic independence and originality of Wong's work make it figure in all this. Particularly that part of his approach in which he contrives to elude the dubious logical schemes of the international style and to retain the bonds with local traditions. A bond maintained in a few characteristics in the representation of regionalist suggestions delegated to few but important touches within his more complex architectonic discourse, in which he accepts many of the positive values of the international approach. Lighter and less engaged is Wong's approach to works solidly anchored to a specific destination and to local use.

This is the case, for example, of circles like the Raffles Marina or the Republic of Singapore Yacht Club, all aspects of which were grouped under a theme. As if in some sort of circumscribed game in which the playful and recreational factor influences the design of the architecture in an nth correspondence between function and result. The centrality of function, moreover, reveals a school of thought and an approach to planning to which Wong's generation is fatally bound. The functionalist approach is in perfect harmony with the world of geometry which Wong infused in his architecture. As in the prevalence of rectangular or square-based prism which, at worst, can be articulated in a "C" arrangement, or be distributed over the territory and then connected by pathways which are

more and more rectilinear and homogeneous from the geometrical viewpoint. And it is perhaps the two works of architecture mentioned, strangely enough those most closely connected with their natural context, that have been given the less functional spatial matrices, even though they have been assigned a much more contrapuntal than leading role in the compositional scheme. In Wong's work the connection with the laws of nature, with the world of non-Euclidean geometry, can rather be found in how he and his collaborators try to control the rhythmical element. A highly important element in his buildings, this rhythm is often present precisely because of his propensity to move his façades through ribbing and openings, all of them in order to determine the rhythmical sequence. The same criterion governs the logic behind vertical succession and punctuation, which Wong fully explores in his tall buildings.

In addition to Wong's importance on the international architectural scene, we must also draw attention to the way his original, independent and passionate work breaks with the lack of homogeneity of contemporary architecture in Singapore. This instils Wong's work with a strange "maieutic" relationship to the architecture in this geographical region.

The interdisciplinary approach and technology

It is for another element that the international approach is presented as an example and reference point for a methodological contribution

to architecture: this is the more specifically productional and professional aspect of the project. This way of working is, moreover, perfectly in harmony with the emergence of a highly qualified and efficient "design machine". Little by little, the architectural studio has been transformed into a larger and larger company and it ends by occupying the very object of their work: the whole skyscraper.

The technologies relative to the production of projects and especially the figures that turn around this product gradually multiply in more and more numerous and articulated teams, which approach the elements with the full competence that constitutes the client's best guarantee. If this method is unable to guarantee good architecture, it is certainly able to put up buildings of the very highest quality from the functional and technological viewpoint. This way of operating has compelled the rest of the world to align itself with this standard, and to guarantee the "product" especially in the case of large-scale works in which the dimensions of the project potentially puts the local studio in competition with big international structures. The advantage of a widespread improvement in constructions comes into competition with a reality in which increasingly the more specifically architectonic value of a work is considered as little more than an "added value" which, though important, is not decisive.

The organisational set-up of Alfred Wong Partnership is such as to guarantee clients the kind of organisational/quality standards associated with a major Anglo-Saxon style firm, while retaining (and therefore adding) all the considerable contributions of architectural awareness that Wong is certainly unwilling to give up.

Interdisciplinary work groups and projects that simultaneously take on architectural (composition, spatiality, materials) and technological/structural matrices are geared, for instance, to the graphic artistry and high-speed sleight of hand in sketching out designs that characterise Ang Choon Kiat. The interaction among these various values is therefore controlled from the very beginning and the choices progressively intertwine in a strongly integrated process in which the quality of the "project produced" is established as the prime and irremissible aim. This is the case of the studies conducted in the wind tunnel, which made it possible to set up a system for the utilization of wind for natural ventilation, a technique later used for the Singapore Polytechnic. Or, even more daringly, in the National Heritage Board, one of Wong's most interesting recent works in which, in order to safeguard the value of the works of art stocked there, a series of sophisticated controls of the environment, the weather, safety, and fire-prevention methods are integrated with an "intelligent building" of the very first order.

It is in this logical framework that one must consider Wong's recent collaboration with big international studios, like HOK, specialized in technological, structural, and installation planning. Context and function, the originating motivations of architecture, produce that "honesty and diversity" that Wong himself states are the noble intention of his work. His collaboration with important international structures has led Wong to acknowledge the innovations in terms of idiom and especially of technology to be found in the work of other professional circles. An approach, which contains a great lesson of attention and of love for the discipline of planning: to put at the base of everyday operations the constant will to learn in a path that his own works of architecture indicate, when interpreted in an historical perspective.

An extraordinary Client

Singapore is capable of rebuilding its own architecture just twenty-years after it was first constructed, drawing on a process of urban renewal involving the demolition of smooth-running buildings to be replaced by new designs more carefully gauged to functional-market requirements.

The economic, geographic and strategic-commercial dimension of Singapore is such that up to now Wong's entire activity has been completely taken up by projects for this "city-state". As if for Wong Singapore as a whole had been transformed into a single extraordinary client. And the architect has responded to this call with works which, for importance and visibility, have also substantially contributed to the transformation of these places. Works like the Robinson Point tower with their vertical design, manage to redefine the whole urban skyline.

The regional "bond" is transformed into a resource through architecture which, owing to its importance and connotations, goes far beyond the geographical confines of the place. The significance in dimensional and strategic terms of Wong's various operations recomposes the system of urban triangulation, distributing throughout the territory the important professional contribution of a studio that has accompanied the growth and development of Singapore since the end of the war.

Works

Marco Polo Hotel
Singapore, 1968-1974

Before being renamed the Marco Polo by the present owner, the original building was known as Hotel Malaysia for which our firm was the Architects in 1968. The total accommodation at that time was 300 Guestrooms.

It was at that time the first modern Hotel of international standard in Singapore. Thus, it was the fore-runner in the 1st Phase development of our Tourist Industry. During the years to follow, many more hotels were built which help to put Singapore well and truly on the tourist map.

The design for the new extension of 308 rooms were commissioned by the new owners after we had carried out some renovation works in the old building to suit their latest requirements.

The original building accommodates 300 Guestrooms in two parallel curved blocks facing the interception of Tanglin Road and Holland Road.

Attached to the rear of this was the largest banqueting Hall in Singapore at that time, accommodating some 1,800 Guests. Car Parking was on ground level surrounding the Hotel.

After the Ownership of the Hotel changed hands and internal refurbishing was done in 1974, we were commissioned to study the technical feasibility of an extension facing Grange Road providing an additional 308 Guestrooms.

The public rooms had to be enlarged and redecorated, but the general layout of the ground floor remains similar to the original concept.

Thus, the entry point of the Hotel is still under the curved marquee although the lobby itself has been enlarged and the Reception area deepened to provide the necessary space appropriate for the increased number of guests.

To maintain a high standard of service, new service-lifts attached to enlarged service areas have been introduced in order to cater to the total complement of Guestrooms which is now doubled in numbers.

A new kitchen and an enlarged service area have been added to the rear of the original block, and at roof level, these areas have been extensively landscaped and now form part of the deck area of the enlarged Swimming Pool.

An increased number of Car Parks up to some 218 are now largely accommodated in a semibasement although short-term car parking is still provided in front of the Hotel entrance.

Extensive landscaping in line with Singapore's Garden City image has been used to complement the existing surroundings of the Hotel which are well endowed with roadside trees.

Opening page,
the original wing
of the hotel (1968)
and its extension,
The Grange Wing
(designed in 1980)
as it stands today.

Below,
exterior corner shot.

Opposite page,
detail of the external
sun shades that provide
an articulated and
functional facade.

Opposite page,
detail of the external
sun shades that provide
an articulated and
functional facade.

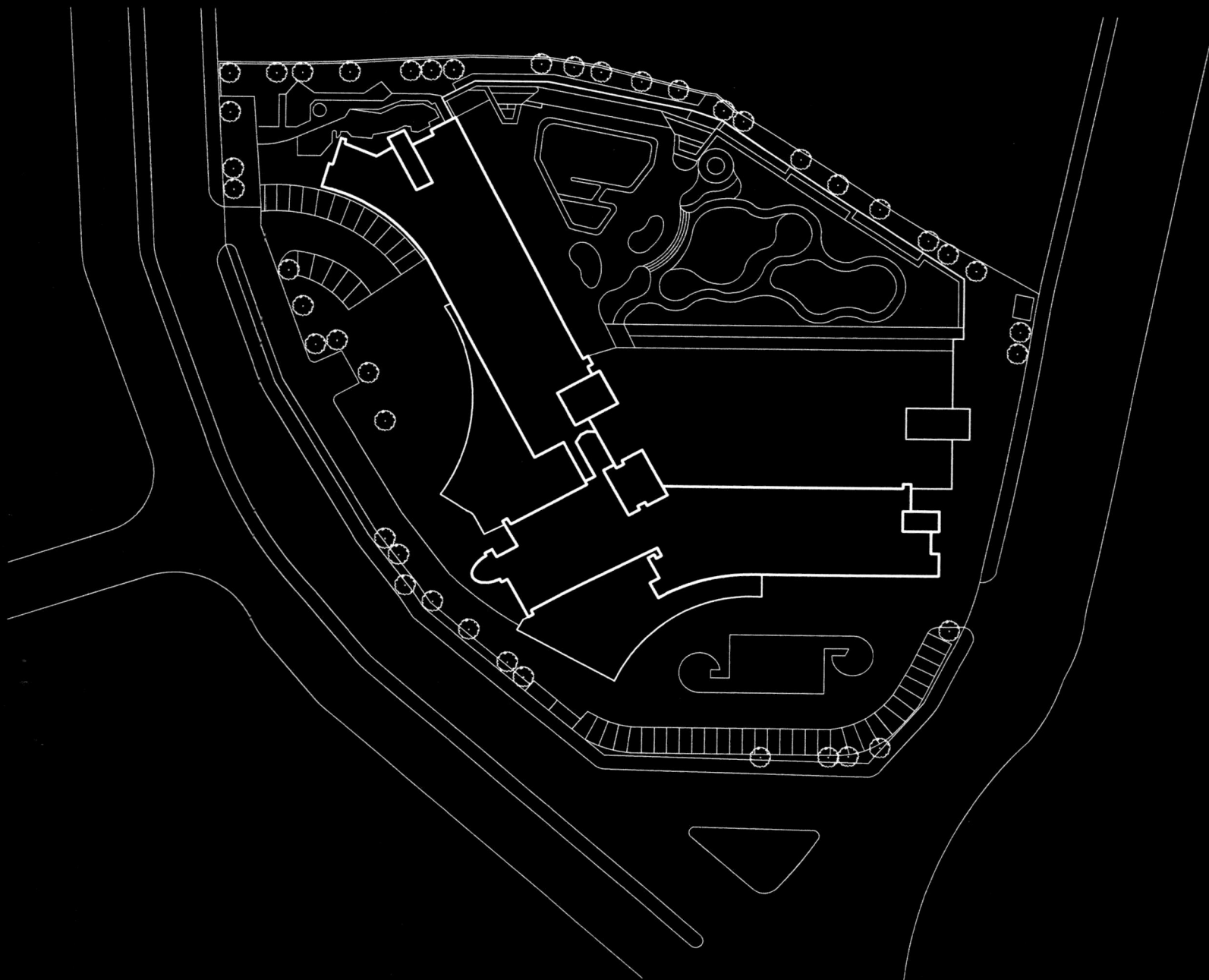

Opposite page,
site plan.

Below, view of new
extension wing that
creates a corner that
folds around a central
courtyard and
recreational area for the
guests, and the original
lobby (now refitted by
its new owners) as
designed by AWP
architects.

Singapore Polytechnic
Singapore, 1979

In February 1983, the Singapore Institute of Architects announced that the 1983 Design Award in the Institution category has been won by the Singapore Polytechnic.

The site for the Polytechnic campus comprised of 327,726 square meters and the total built-on area of buildings total up to 74,320 square meters

When the first academic session began in May 1978, the total student population was 8,086 of which 4,928 were full-time students. The range of technical courses cover architecture and building, engineering courses such as civil, electrical and electronic, mechanical, marine, structural and production engineering. There is also a special department for nautical engineering, works management and special courses ranging from color television, digital computers, production technology and quality engineering. (There is also a department of nautical studies which is housed in a separate building away from the campus in part of the Port area of Singapore).

The configuration of the site plan is in the form of parallel blocks to achieve the desired orientation since it is a requirement that most of the teaching area will have to be naturally ventilated. These are linked system to linkways which formed quadrangles giving the whole campus a series of open spaces interfacing one group of buildings with the other.

Except for special laboratories, housing equipment that require air conditioning, most of the teaching rooms have been planned for natural ventilation. In the case of the workshop blocks, a special "windscoop" device designed with the aid of wind tunnel testing is used to provide cross ventilation even when a double loaded, i.e. central corridor system is used between workshops.

2.5-meter wide exterior walkways are provided for workshops both for all weather access as well as to provide shade and rain cover to the precast concrete vents and windows which form the side walls of the workshops.

In the case of the teaching blocks a standard unit measuring 48x5 meters is placed at two sides of a quadrangle linked by covered linkways so that natural ventilation can be maintained.

Two large lecture theaters each accommodating 300 persons, equipped with audio/visual aids are air-conditioned and are scheduled for use by the various departments of the Polytechnic. In addition there are four small lecture theaters of 150 persons capacity; and one special theater for 110 persons equipped for electronic demonstrations.

Vertical circulation such as staircases and lifts together with toilet-areas are contained in separate blocks at the nodal points of the linkway system. This is to isolate noise and disturbance as much as possible away from the teaching blocks. The teaching blocks themselves contain only teaching rooms and exit staircases as required under fire regulations.

The administration block situated at the central part of the complex stands on a base which has been designed to be an extension of the site topography. It can be seen in the photographs as a brickface structure which was in fact first built to house the electrical sub-station and the main air conditioning plant which supplies chilled water for the air handling units in the special areas of the campus for which air conditioning is required. (This includes the administration building and the library building opposite, plus certain laboratory areas).

Since the Polytechnic caters to both full-time as well as part-time students, a fairly high "car population" was expected. Accordingly, extensive car parks are planned around the various workshops in order that students and teachers may have reasonable access to and from the car parks not withstanding the extent of the whole complex as well as the dispersion of the various teaching departments.

Opening page,
window detail showing
the brightly painted
corridor fenestration.
These precast concrete
vents and windows
form the side walls
of the workshops.

Below, site plan.

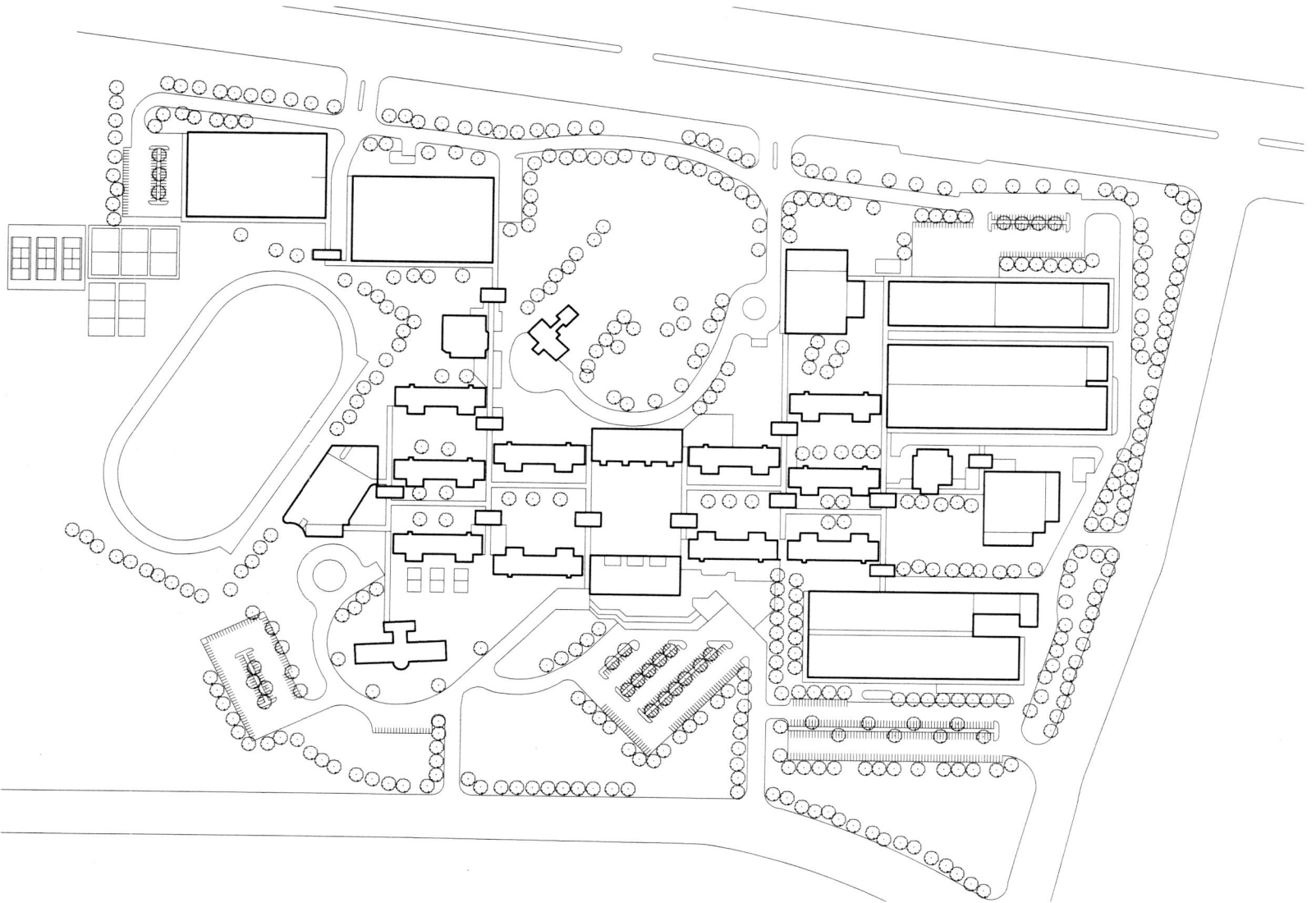

Right, the front
entrance facade to the
library.

Below, a Modernist
courtyard expression;
the plan is in the form
of parallel blocks
connected to a system
of linkways forming
quadrangles.

Next pages, aerial view
of the complex.

Pedestrian prioritised design provides efficient walkways throughout the campus. These exterior walkways provide all-weather access between workshops and provide rain and shade cover.

Inside of a lecture
theatre.

St. Joseph's Institution
Malcom Road, Singapore, 1987-1995

St Joseph's Institution consists of a collection of buildings built on a multi-levelled site that dictated much of the conceptual planning. As a result, the final arrangement is an interesting and feasible solution for the school as a whole. The classroom blocks, administration, assembly hall and workshops are located to the rear on the higher terrain to the west. The natural terrain of the land extends down towards the north forming a secluded pocket of land on which the brothers' quarters are sited. The Chapel is located between the quarters and the school premises, conveniently accessible to the school itself, but located far enough away from the noisier activities. The playing field runs the full length of these buildings providing an interface to Malcolm Road.

Such a collection of buildings with numerous varied usage provides an excellent opportunity to express each function in a sculptural and individualistic manner, whilst still retaining architectural cohesion amongst the variation.

The concept and design of the school was the result of close coordination between the school management committee and the Architects. The school had a list of twenty-five items comprising of artifacts and momentos from the original St Joseph's Institution at Bras Basah Road, which were to be displayed at strategic points of the new school to serve as a reminder of the long history of the school and provide a sense of continuity between the old premises and the new.

In addition, there are also various art works such as an oil painting of the martyrdom of the Christian brothers in Philippines in World War II which is given a prominent position in the main concourse of the school.

Various ideas and suggestions were contributed by old boys of SJI who requested that as far as possible some features of the old school should be incorporated in the design of the new.

In addition to the design of the interior which had to incorporate the art works and artifacts, part of the building such as the Chapel included art works from dedicated and creative designers such as Mr. Ho Kok Hoe, who designed and fabricated the stained glass panel of the chapel depicting the risen Christ. It is more than just a stained glass window, as the glass pieces making up the panel are in fact solid glass blocks of irregular shapes, which were assembled to give a scintillating impact as the focal point of the Chapel.

Another old boy, Mr Koh Boon Piang, who is himself a trained graphic designer has hand drawn the lettering of the 14 stations of the cross which is framed in glass and suspended away from the glass windows. This is lit by natural light in the day and built-in artificial lighting at night.

Rev Bro. Joseph McNally contributed the statue of St. John Baptist De La Salle which is the focus of the curved elevation linking the two main classroom blocks of the school.

Even when working on the development of the plans using the MOE's provisions as a basic starting point, the provision of a concourse as the "heart" of the school has resulted in a very usable space for exhibitions, lectures and small gatherings of students for discussion groups away from the more rigid and standardized interior of a typical classroom.

Overall, the major objective was to ensure that the school buildings should be more than glass and concrete and the design of both the exterior as well as the interior with its contents should reflect the spirit of the Christian brothers school as far as possible.

A more obvious feature of this is the replica of one old statue of the old St. Joseph's Institution which serves as a pavilion under which the foundation stone is laid and also forms the back-drop to a replica of St John Baptist De La Salle which is a full-size copy of the original, still located at the old school in Bras Basah Road.

Opening page,
the chapel is in a
cruciform plan in four
semi-circular vaults
forming curved ceilings
within.

Right, most of the site
was multi-layered and
with a certain amount
of site formation, an
interesting layout for
the school was feasible.

The dominant feature
facing the entrance is a
replica of one arch bay
of the old SJI, where a
reproduction of the
founder's statue is
located.

Opposite page,
site plan.

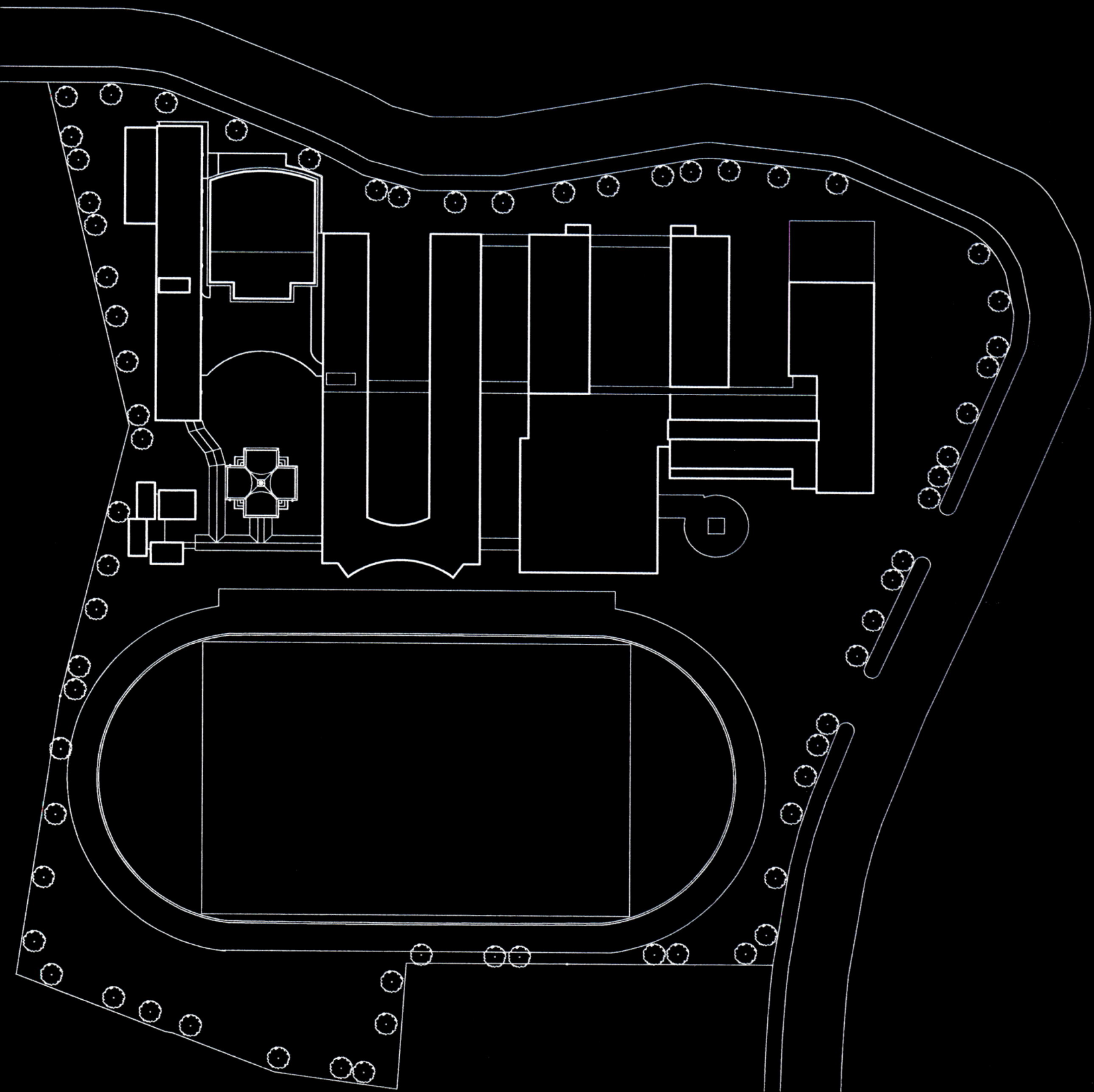

Opposite page,
semi-circular arches are
reminiscent of the
school's original
building nearer the
center of Singapore.

Below, the ceiling
of the Chapel.

Odeon Towers
Singapore, 1992

The twenty-three-storey tower is a tribute to intelligent and buildable design. A single modular grid of 1.3 meters is observed by most building components including the curtain walling system, the granite stonework, the GRC cladding and glass screens, right down to the metal ceilings, lighting fixtures and air-conditioning linear diffusers. These were designed to be prefabricated or precast off site for an uncomplicated and rapid construction.

Sited in the fringe of the civic and cultural district, the tower exploits the best views of the city by spanning the full width of the site. The column-free space wraps around the core on three sides thereby offering an uninterrupted vista for its occupants as well as liberating the office space. In keeping with the classical approach to big and tall buildings, considerable attention is lavished on their relationship with the ground and on the hierarchy of spaces. In order to connect the tower with the city block in which it stands, a porticoed perimeter was created which, in its turn, delimits a small public "courtyard" that gives access to the Hall of the construction. The role of emphasizing the progression towards the top of the tower has been delegated to the overhanging elements on the facade. Notably, its ingenious modular coordination and standardization systems won a Certificate of Merit at the CIDB's Best Buildable Design Awards in 1992.

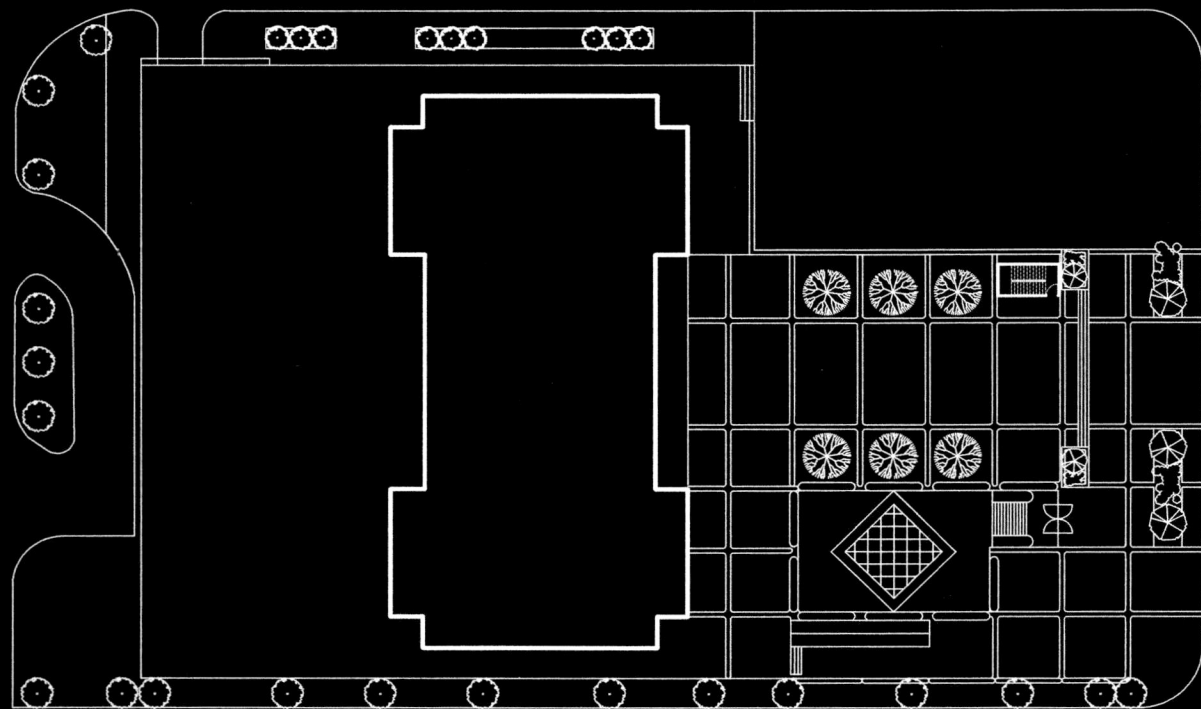

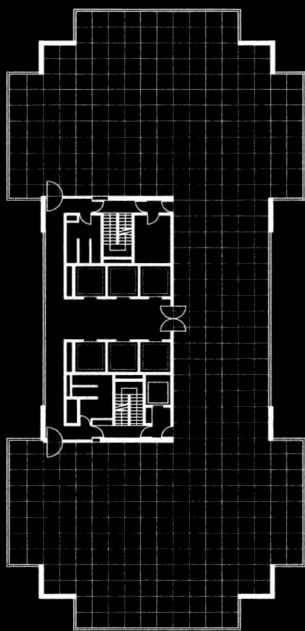

Sited opposite Raffles
Hotel, the building
soars twenty three
storeys above
a grand colonnade.

Opposite page, the
glass pyramid makes an
elegant and effective
lightwell for the
restaurant below.

Below, the grand
colonnade plaza of
tapering columns and
vaulted ceilings.

Next pages,
detail of the elegant
glass mullions.

Raffles Marina
Tuas West Drive, Singapore, 1992

The site, with a planning designation for recreational (sea-sports) use, was awarded to our clients further to their successful competitive trend to develop the land, based on AWP's design concept.

The site is 4.2 hectares and is located on reclaimed seafront land on the western extremity of Singapore Island. It has views over the Straights of Johore, with its fishing "Kaylongs", and Malaysia is clearly visible beyond.

The development can be best described as a "Resort Marina", designed in an evocative tropical yet contemporary style, low, with strong horizontal lines and large over hanging eaves, shading the airy verandahs and colonnades.

The facilities in the club includes three restaurants, 500-seat Ballroom, Function Rooms, Bali lagoon pool with swim up bar, water falls, slides and hot Jacuzzi pool, Gym/Fitness Center, Tennis Courts, squash courts, Cinema, eight-lane Bowling Alley Billiards Room and 20 Guestrooms and suites.

For the boaters there is a fixed break water sheltering some 165 walk-on berths, accommodating craft from 40' cruisers up to the 200'+ Mega Yachts of the rich and famous! Additionally there is a drystack boathouse with mechanized system of stacking for 304 boats, of up to 35'. The construction of the breakwater requires special engineering methods and the use of the mechanized stacking system is a first in Singapore. The Club also has extensive facilities for hauling out and launching craft for repairs and maintenance.

Opening page, detail of the glass mullions inside the club house.

Left, entrance to Raffles Marina. The marina is designed with large overhanging pitched roofs, reminiscent of the features of earlier Singapore buildings.

Below, site plan.

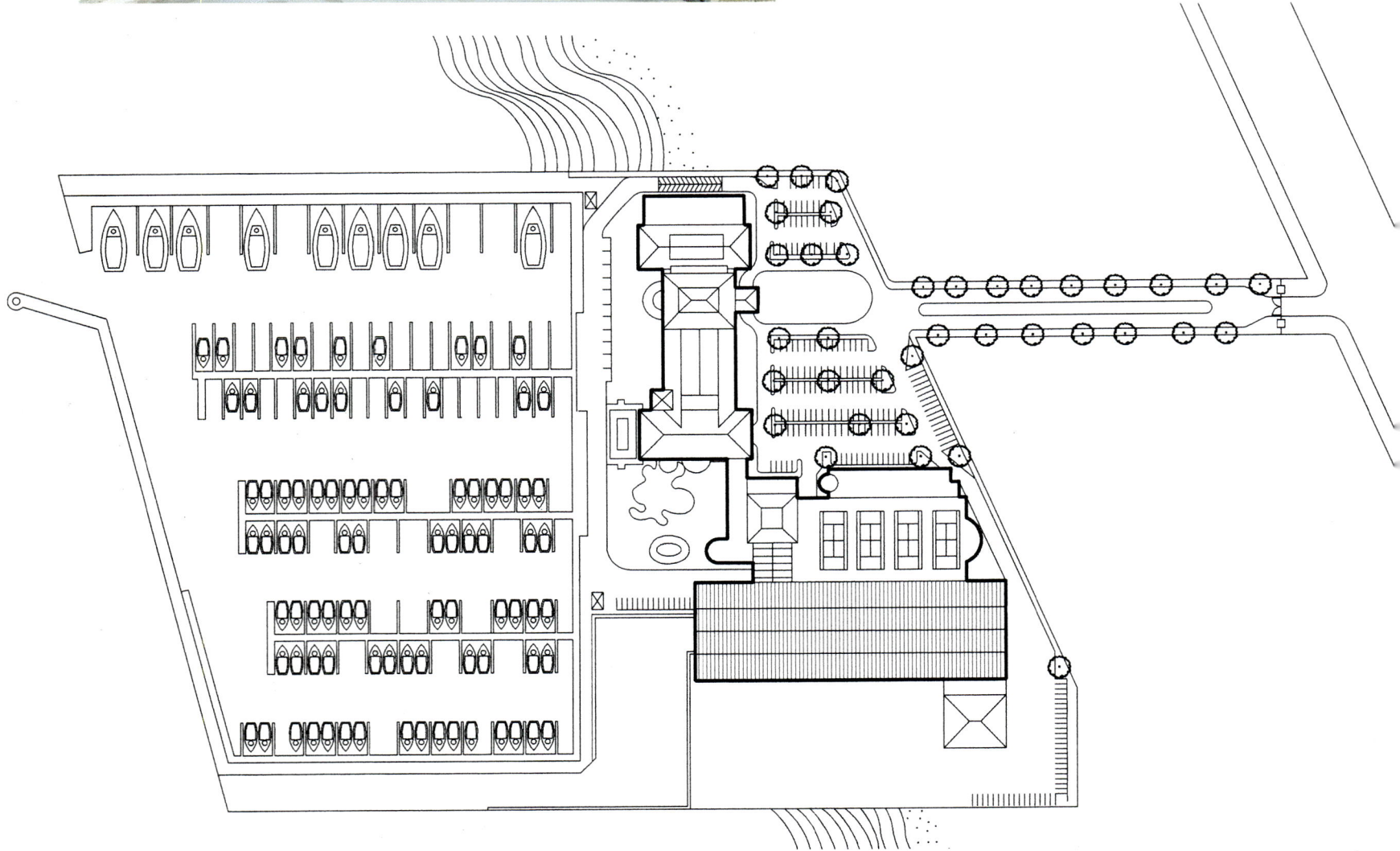

Right, inside the boat stacking shed which houses a mechanised stacking system, the first in Singapore.

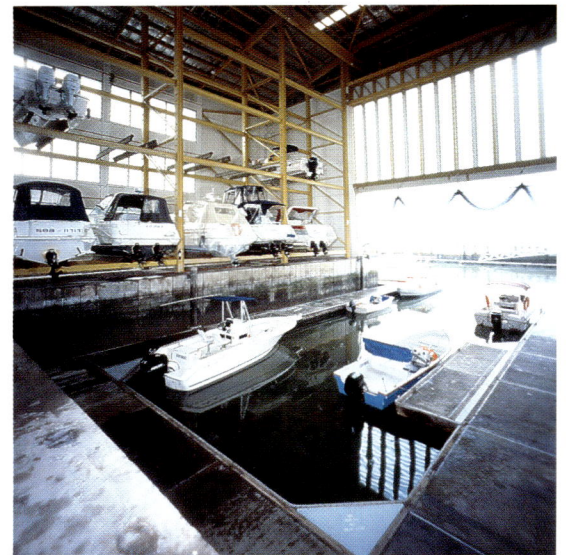

Poolside view.
Beside the normal
clubhouse facilities,
there are berths for
165 boats and a
boatstacking shed
with a capacity
of 304 boats.

Next pages,
the marina from the
waterfront is situated
on a parcel of 42,374
square meters of sea
front land at Tuas.

The interior of the
clubhouse is consciously
monumental and
almost theatrical in
style.

The plush interior
of the clubhouse.

Keppel Distripark for the Port of Singapore Authority
Singapore, 1993

Alfred Wong Partnership was appointed as Design Consultant to the Engineering Division of Port of Singapore Authority, a group that included both engineers and architects and who were the Project Architects for the design of the proposed PSA Distripark. This consists of a complex of buildings covering a total gross floor area of 137,338 square meters or 1.48 million square feet.

Completed in 1993, Keppel Distripark comprises of four blocks of 2-storey Container Freight Station (CFS) Building, one block of 4-storey office building, stacking yards, chassis parks and other related facilities.

To create the maximum area of unobstructed floor-space, the roofing system was in the form of a suspended space frame structure. For example, the larger buildings of 96x120 meters was roofed over by a series of cable-suspended pyramidal roofs on six masts or columns.

The external walls of the Distripark in the form of composite metal cladding, customed designed as part of the crossbracing panels is integral with the structural system and at the same time giving a distinctive pattern to the elevations.

The design of the Keppel Distripark thus reflects the "hi-tech" aspects both of construction technology as well as the modern methods of container port operation for which Singapore is well known.

At the same time, in view of the importance of the site location, the design of the masts and suspension structure gives a festive appearance when seen from the surrounding roads and the devices of noise-screening as well as visual screening from existing residential development are also incorporated into the overall planning.

At the mid-point of the linear elevations is the Administration building which is in the form of a "glass cube" structure, surrounded by terraces with extensive landscaping to provide an interesting contrast to the formal geometric form of the storage buildings.

Opening page,
Keppel Distripark is the
largest container
freight in Asia.

Right, nighttime view.

Below, site plan.

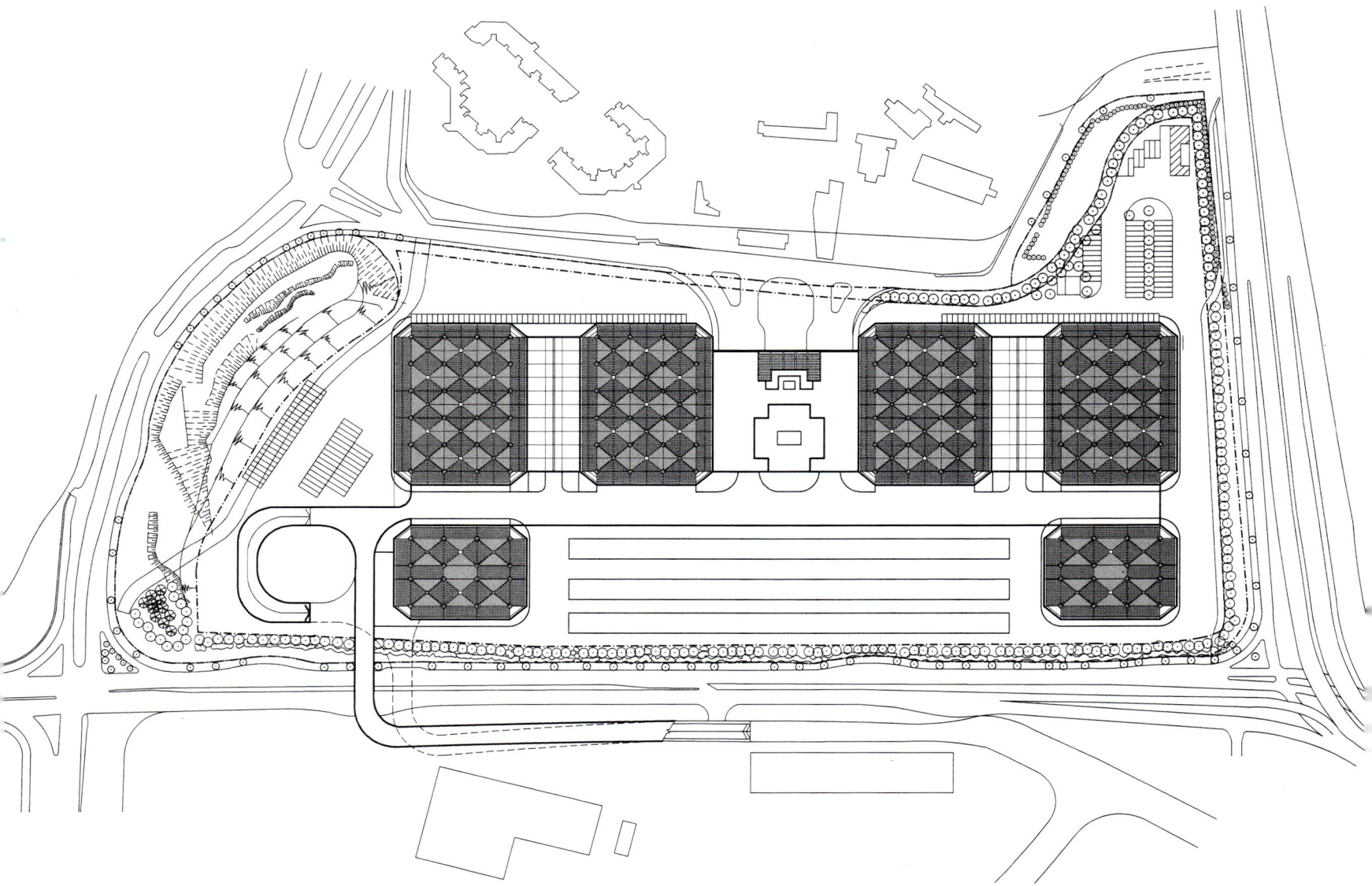

The Distripark's
137,338 square meters
occupy five individual
blocks.

Right, the suspension structure for the roof gives a column free storage space to the terminal.

Below, the external walls, equal to the height of an eight-storey building, use composite metal cladding, custom designed as part of the cross bracing panels.

58

The external panels are both structural and decorative giving a nautical theme to the aesthetics.

Singapore Tourist Board Headquarters
Singapore, 1995

This project was the resulte of a tender award by the Singapore Tourist Promotion Board.

The project consists of a 13-storey Office Block facing onto an internal courtyard garden with a 3-storey Basement Car Parks. The main frontage at Grange Road will have a 2-storey high colonnaded structure accommodating exhibition spaces, public function rooms and lecture theaters all of which will be used by the Board for its promotional activities.

The architectural design makes use of a formation of pitch roofs set at various levels to give the building a distinctive identity recalling some aspects of the traditional buildings of early Singapore. A distinctive feature of the facade is the stylized "traveller's palm" motif skillfully etched into the colonnade structure conceptually derived from the client's brief to give the building its own uniquely traditional identity.

The building will be fully equipped with the latest building automation, sometimes described as an "intelligent building" to give the optimum functional efficiency to all the office floors and covers the provision of building security, energy conserving provisions, and total design with user friendly aspects as one of the prime requirements.

Opposite page, detail of the stepping of the roof line.

Right, overall view of the Singapore Tourist Promotion Board before the surrounding buildings were constructed.

Site plan.

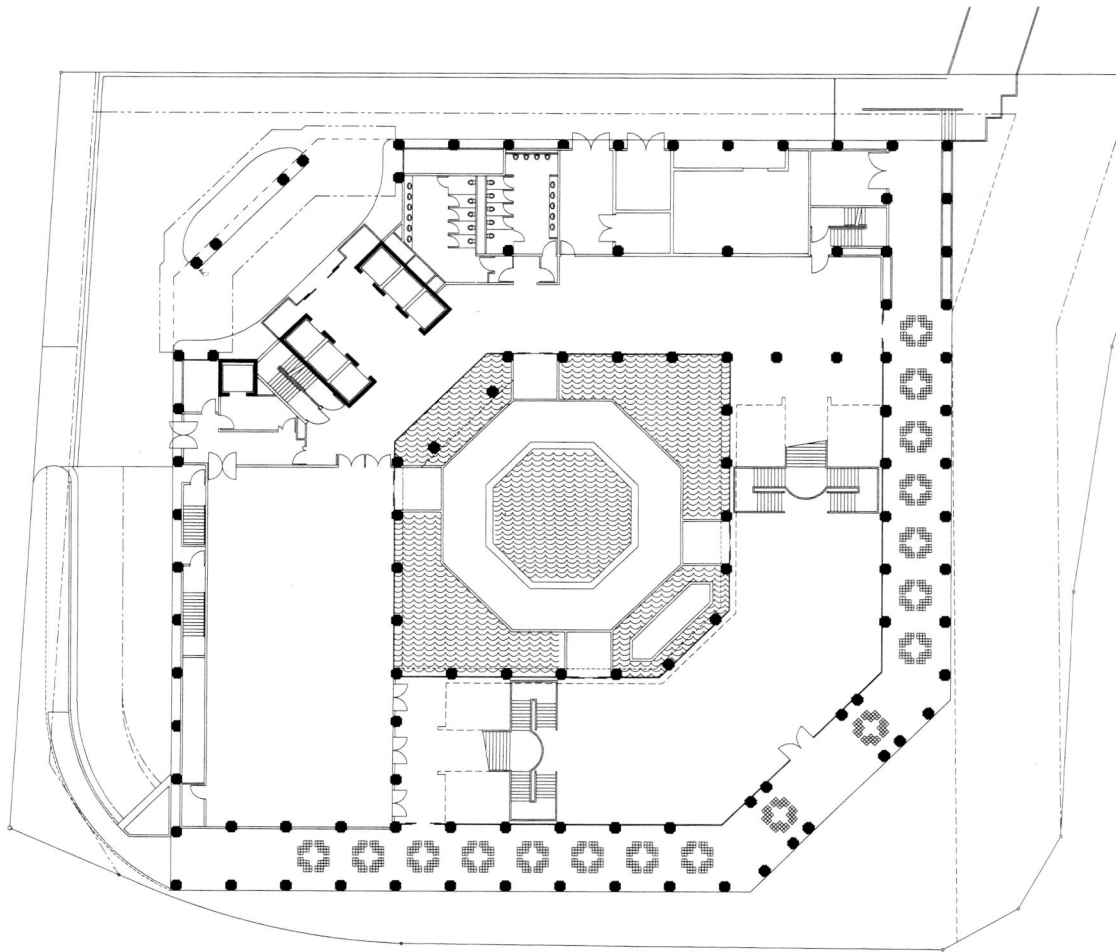

Plan of a typical floor.

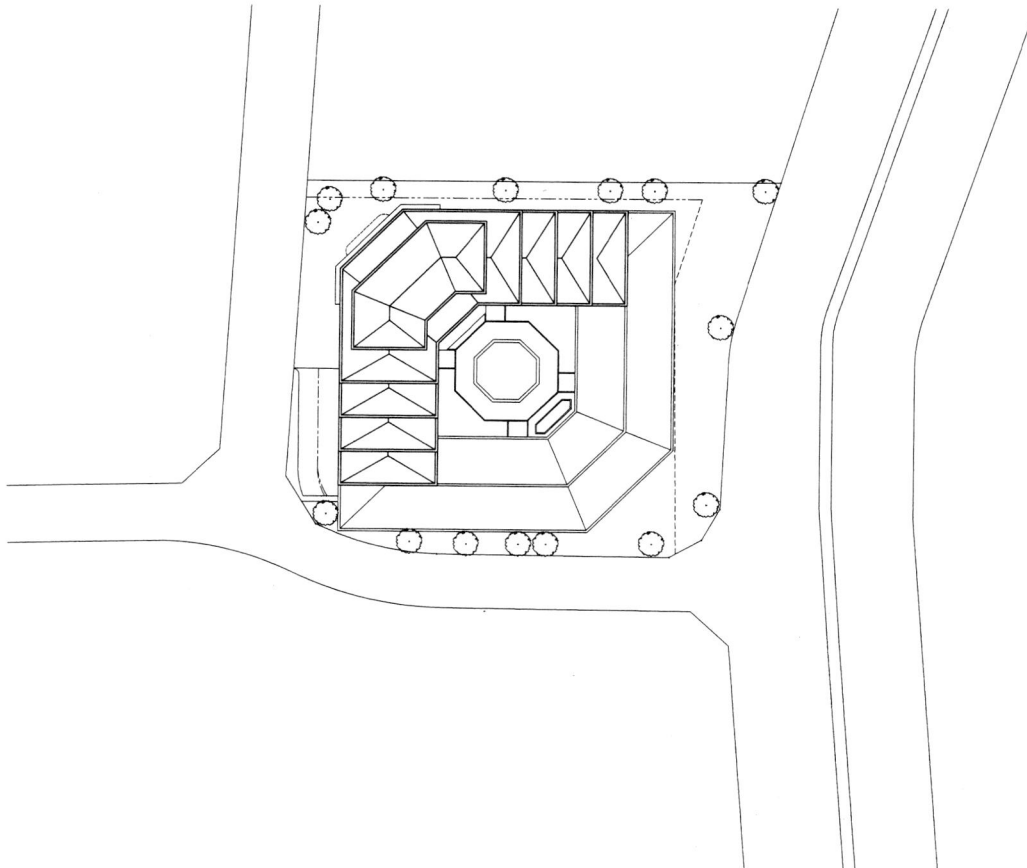

Plan of the first floor.

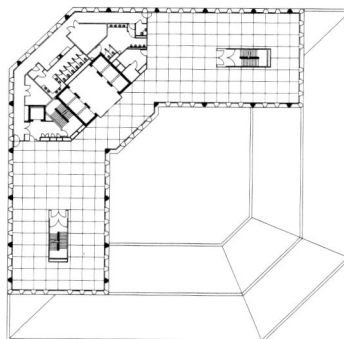

Opposite page,
nighttime view.

Below, a Lily pond is the central feature of the landscaped courtyard.

Bottom, detail of the Travellers' palm motif designed by Alfred Wong Partnership specifically for the Client.

Right, colonnade surrounding the internal courtyard showing the specially designed motif derived from the "Travellers' Palm", one of Singapore's trademarks.

Reception lobby and
staircase.

Schering Plough Pharmaceutical Manufacturing Facilities
Tuas West Drive, Singapore, 1997

Alfred Wong Partnership were the local architects for this Plant and Process Design. (The leading consultants were John Brown E & C, Bridgewater N.J.,USA). The massive complex, situated on a ten-hectare site, is the base for the first US pharmaceutical firm to set up manufacturing operations in Singapore. A clean geometrical design evolved through its function and usage. It was precisely the specifically industrial character of the work carried out there that determined the choices made in the composition and the aggregation of volumes. Different constructions distributed throughout the area in question are connected by a system of exterior vehicular and pedestrian paths. The presence of zones for sterile processing or, in any case, the reduced need for windowed sections in the production parts, made it possible to study in greater depth the theme of the modularity and compositional grids of the facades. Pragmatic and efficient, the facilities provided include an administration building, warehouses, production buildings and laboratories with clean rooms, warehouses and a boiler house with auxiliary buildings amounting to twenty-five thousand square meters of gross floor area.

Opening page,
the main entrance
to the complex.

Right, main gatehouse.

Below, site plan.

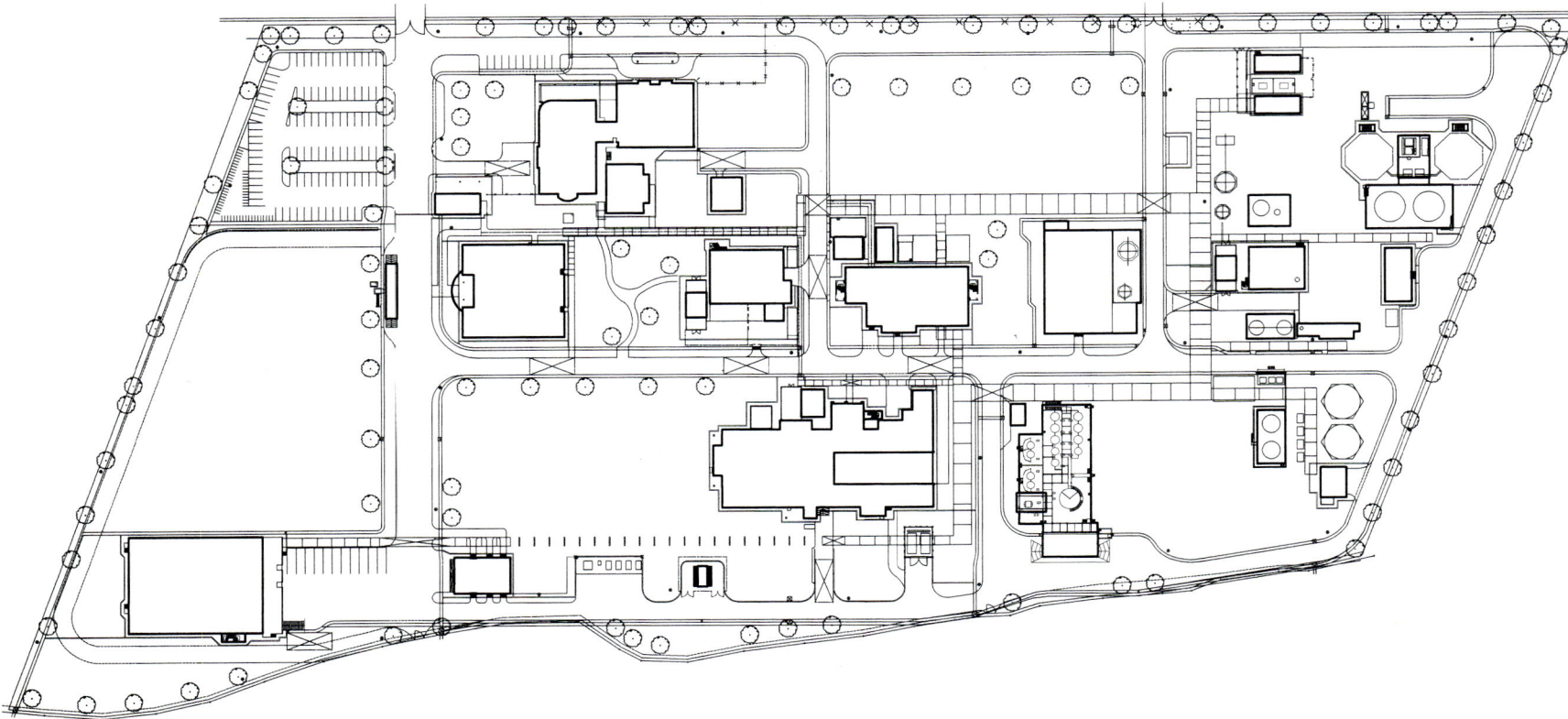

Main administrative
building.

Front entrance of administration building.

Below, view from the centre of the compound showing the ten-hectare site with landscaped grounds.

Next pages, overall view of Schering Plough, the first US pharmaceutical firm to set up operations in Singapore.

Facilities include
administration building,
production buildings
with clean rooms,
laboratories,
warehouses and
a boiler house.

The canteen.

Below, detail
of stairwell.

The National Museums Artifacts Repository (National Heritage Board)
Jurong Port Road, Singapore, 1997

The objective was to reconcile the potentially conflicting operational requirements of the Client into a coherent design representative of the building's function and statement of purpose. The building form is derived from the clear expression of the functional elements of the plan, its circulation requirements and the asymmetrical juxtaposition of their geometric forms, which is emphasized by material contrast and the use of detail.

The critical design concepts for the building were derived from the resolution of the narrow linear site constriction and the contrasting functions required by the National Heritage Board, which ultimately determined the building form. The design had to accommodate the provision of large vehicular delivery, high occupant and visitor security control whilst providing executive offices, viewing galleries/reception, laboratories and extensive specialized artifact storage. Allowance was also required for future expansion with minimal disruption to the operation of the building.

The loading bay, security control building, automation control room and reception are located at the front of the building to minimize circulation requirements. This offers the benefit of immediate building control, reduction of site area lost to circulation and the optimum efficient arrangement for artifact delivery/loading and control. The remaining three storeys above this area consist of the viewing room and offices directly accessed by the sweeping timber spiral staircase and vertical exhibition space or adjacent passenger lift. These areas are elevationally defined by full height glazing and concrete brise soleils which taper to emphasize the aluminium clad conical form which marks the buildings points of entry and houses the reception, spiral staircase and vertical exhibition space. These vertically arranged spaces accessible to the public/visitor with a generally lower security requirement constitutes the head of the building. The head of the building in terms of function and security is separated from the main body of the artifacts repository by a lateral service corridor linked directly to the spiral staircase and passenger lift with access to the central corridor "spine" of the building restricted by security card access. This plan arrangement allows logical and efficient security control of visitors, staff and artifacts.

The 88-meter-long and 32-meter-wide artifacts storage areas form the main body of the building, split by a central corridor linked directly to the goods lift located at the junction with the head of the building and point of security control.

The monolithic form of the 26-meter-high 4-storey storage areas which require environmental control and no daylight is subdivided into three zones by means of the escape/maintenance staircases. As a result of the fire fighting and maintenance access road required at first storey these zones are cantilevered out at second and third storey so valuable storage area is not lost as a result of the first storey setback. In contrast to these aluminium clad volumes, proportioned as "Golden Sections" the oversize storage area setback at first storey is expressed by brickwork divided by exposing the circular concrete columns, with the shadow gap between concealing the syphonic rainwater down pipes and allowing easy maintenance.

The laboratories at fourth storey are set back from the facade line to form a maintenance terrace for the horizontal glazing, which clearly expresses the alternative function behind, dividing the storage areas from the over sailing cantilever of the roof eaves above. The cantilever of the roof serves to unify the composition whilst shading the laboratories from direct sunlight and protecting the facade from "streaking" as result of more polluted rain prevalent in industrial areas. The visual progression of this facade concludes with inverted aluminium cone rising above which floats the geometric form of the aluminium roof, which hovers above the trees marking the buildings presence to the distant observer or arriving visitor.

expresses the spiral
staircase within.

Singapore's National
Museums and galleries.

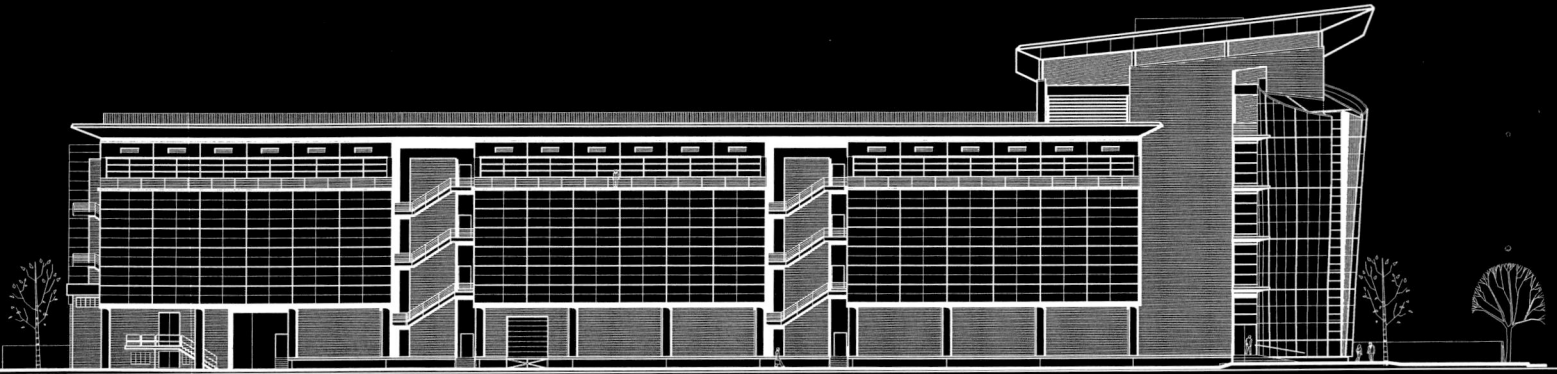

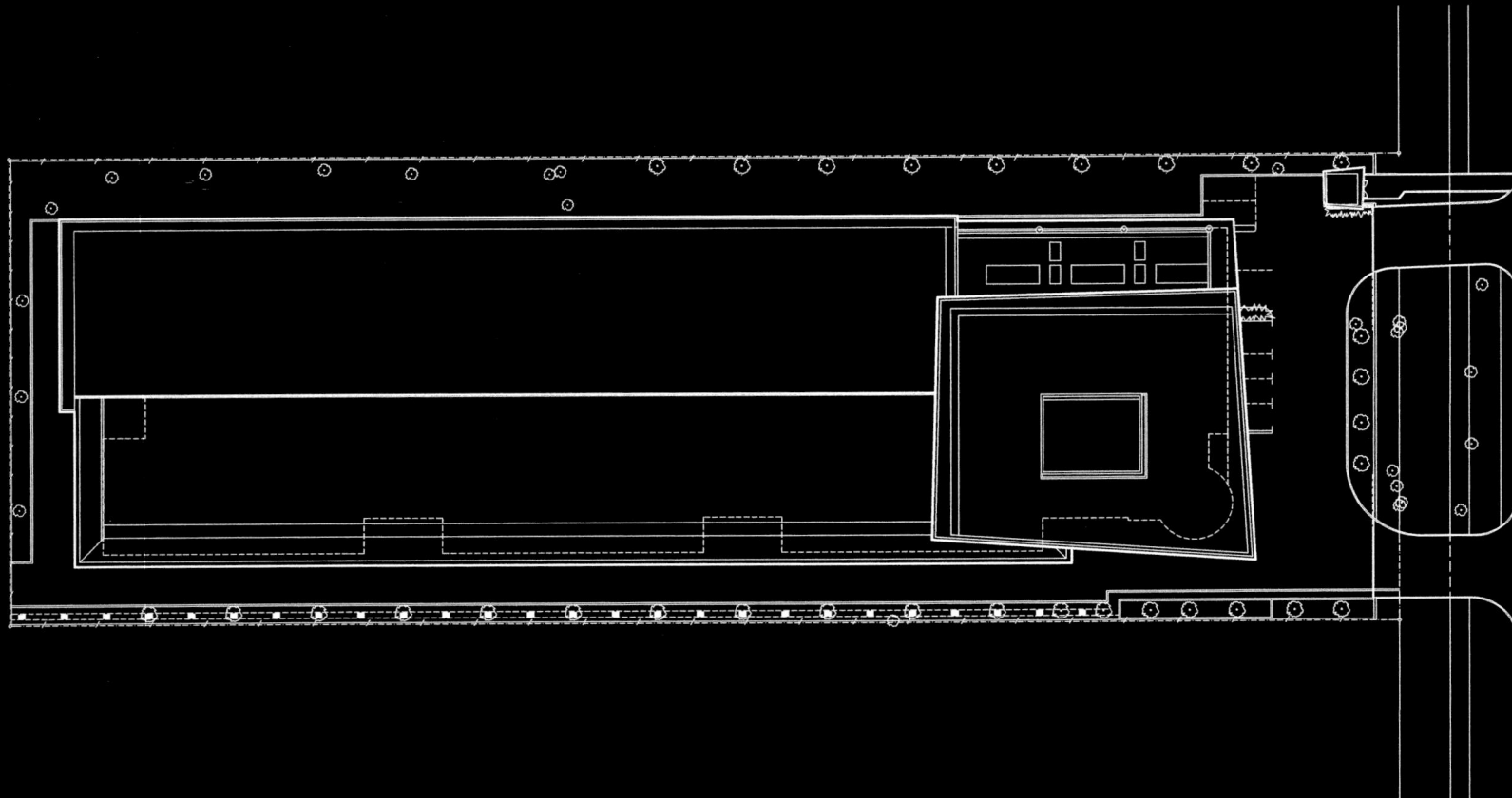

Below, detail of fire
escape stairs.

Opposite page,
detail of the functional
and aesthetic sun
shading to the front
of the building.

Opposite page,
view looking upwards
into the lightwell
of the drum.

Above, stairwell.

Left, the main stairwell
doubles as an exhibition
space for artifacts.

Robinson Point
39 Robinson Road, Singapore, 1997

The Robinson Road project consists of two retail spaces at first storey level below a podium carpark of five storeys. The remaining fifteen storeys form a column-free rental space with a typical central core.

The constraints of the site led to a design with a central core (housing two scissor staircases, six passenger lifts and one fire service lift, as well as toilets, mechanical and electrical shafts and risers). This provided an outer column-free zone to maximize tenancy flexibility. The core was designed to be as economical as possible to maximize net lettable area while providing an appropriately sized lift lobby. Setting out involved careful calculations for smoke stop lobby sizes, stair widths and shaft sizes to ensure all authority requirements were met while minimizing non-lettable space. This resulted in a very efficient ratio of lettable to non-lettable space for the building owner.

The tower design (from the sixth to the twenty-first storey) utilizes a symmetrical perimeter plan with all four elevations consisting of central curtain walling strips of double glazed, low emissivity glass to reduce direct solar heat gain. The silicon sealant on the horizontal joints, and stainless steel channels on the vertical joints, emphasize the verticality of the central facade.

The building is capped by a four-sided pyramidal roof (16x16 m in plan) with a pitch of 35 degrees. The aim of the skylight was to provide a proper design solution for the concealment of the roof plant and satisfactorily complete the "fifth" elevation. The space frame is capped with a 16-meter mast which led to the naming of the building "Robinson Point". The skylight and mast form a unique silhouette on the Singapore skyline, especially when illuminated at night.

The front podium elevation closely reflects the neighboring listed TAS building with a continuation of the classical language. The main entrance elevation is the focal point of the podium, with the main building signage at fifth storey level being visible but no obtrusive.

The external color scheme of blue, silver, and white is carried through into the internal details and finishes including the building signage. The color schemes for all building elements including finishes for the internal aluminium, the granite finishes internal signage, toilet tiles and paintwork were carefully coordinated to ensure compatibility.

Opening page, nighttime view of Robinson Point lit up.

Left, Robinson Point in context with the greater built environment of Singapore's CBD.

Opposite page, front elevation from Robinson Road at dusk with glimpse of lift lobby and retail premises on the ground floor.

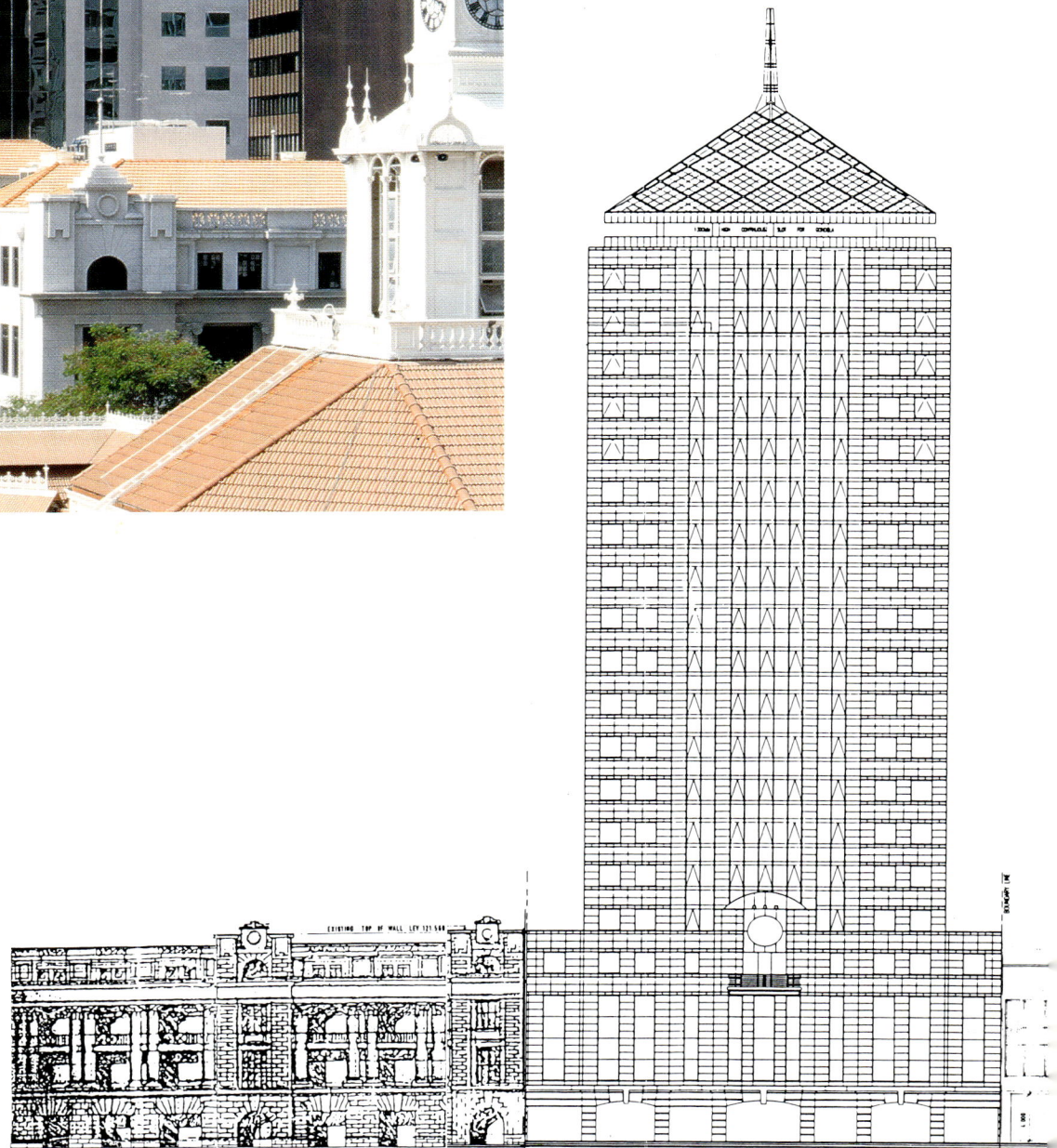

North-west elevation.

Below, plan of a typical
floor.

Right, lift lobby.

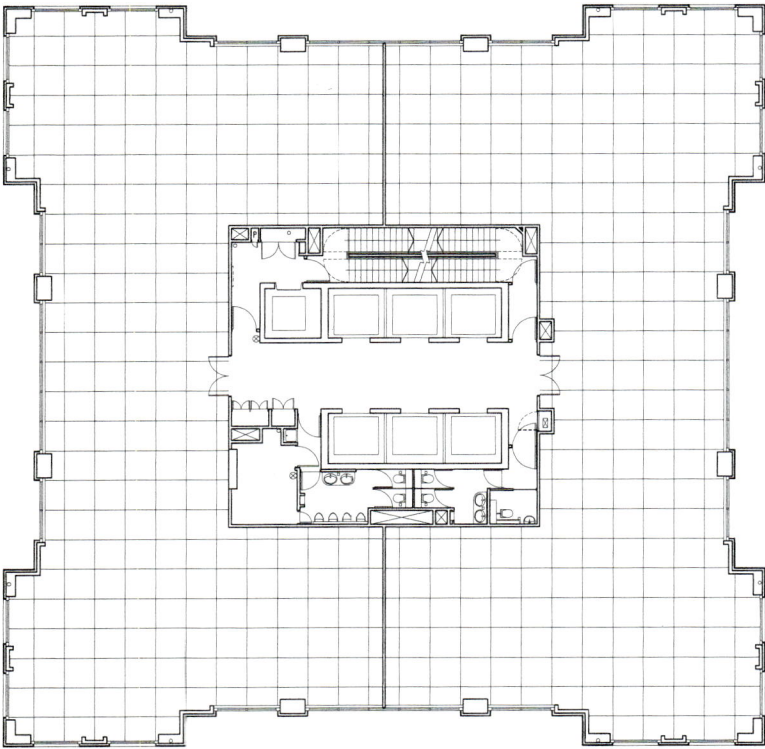

Republic of Singapore Yacht Club
Singapore, under construction-1999

The Republic of Singapore Yacht Club, established in 1834 and Singapore's oldest, is now building a completely new, state of the art facility, on reclaimed land adjacent to West Coast Park. We have been developing the design with a number of successive committees, which changes on an annual basis, bringing with it new ideas, all wrought into the final design which is presently underway on site.

The new club will comprise walk-on pontoon berthing, for 175 boats up to 80', protected from the open sea by a floating wave attenuator. Boaters will be able to take provisions right up to their boats on motorized buggies. A "racked" dry boat storage structure will provide further capacity for 300 boats up to 40'.

The club will have a 7,500-square-meter Clubhouse, which has been designed in a contemporary, nautical idiom. The roof of the clubhouse is distinctive, both as a modern reflection of the traditional minangkabau roof form and as a metaphor for yachts sails, and will present a readily identifiable landmark for returning yachtsmen.

The clubhouse, which has two restaurants, gym/fitness center, function & business facilities as well as 40 guestrooms and suites, is arranged in courtyard fashion, centered around a swimming pool. The pool deck extends into the circulation and activity spaces of the club, allowing members to take advantage consistent warmth of the tropical climate. An entrance foyer which looks over the pool and marina beyond will be the location of a permanent exhibition, encapsulating the clubs long history and heritage.

Opposite page, perspective view of Singapore's oldest yacht club warranted a prolific design to create a state of the art marina and clubhouse. Facilities for 180 wet berths and 300 dry berths are catered for.

Below, site plan.

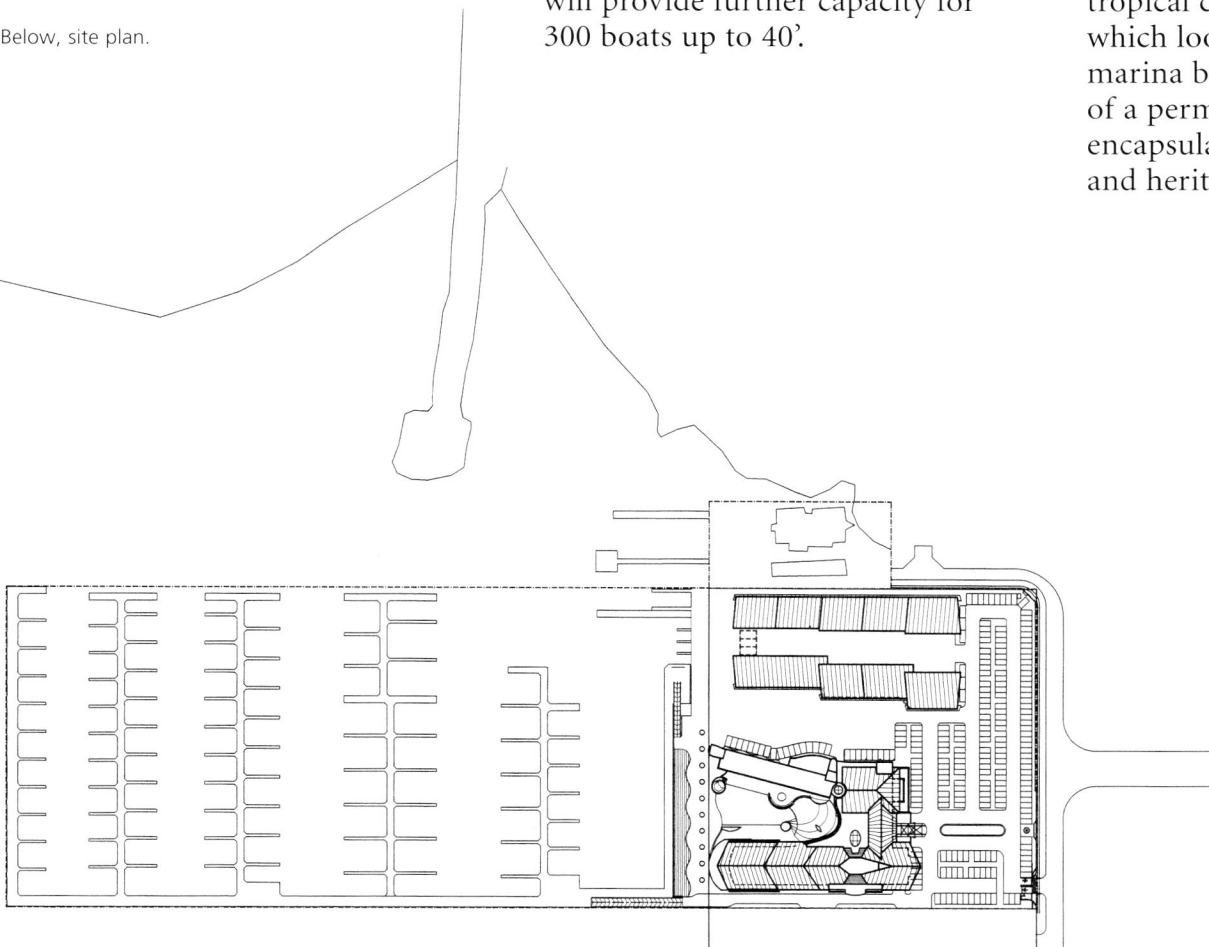

Perspective view of the new Yacht Club.

Below, cross and longitudinal sections.

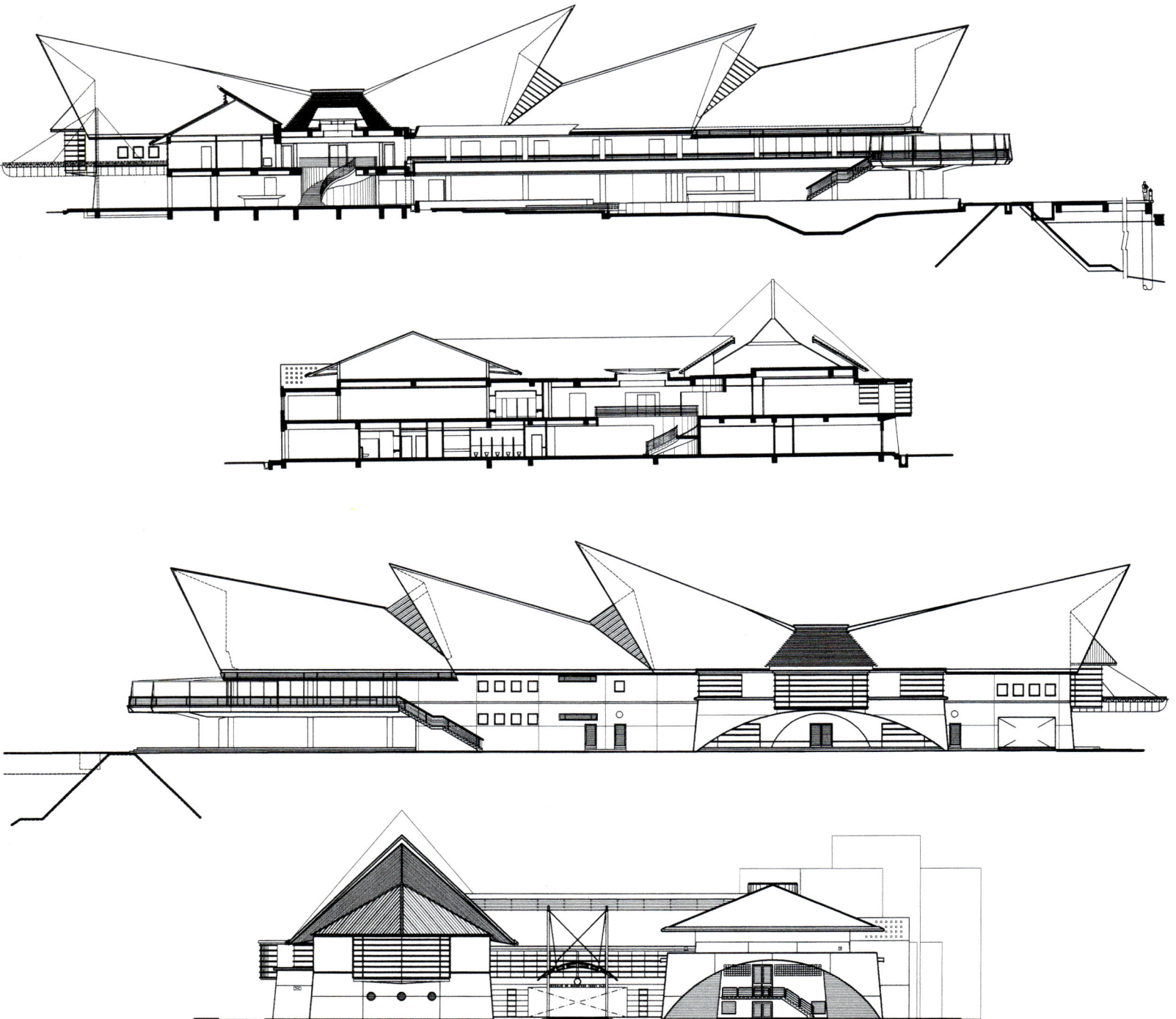

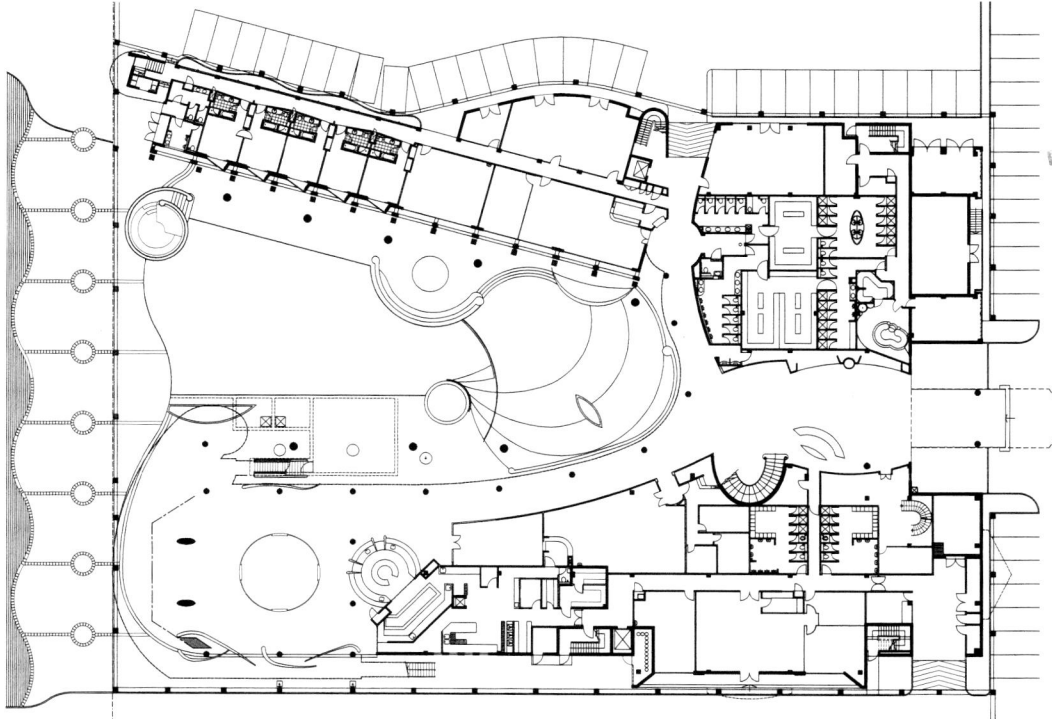

Plan of the third floor.

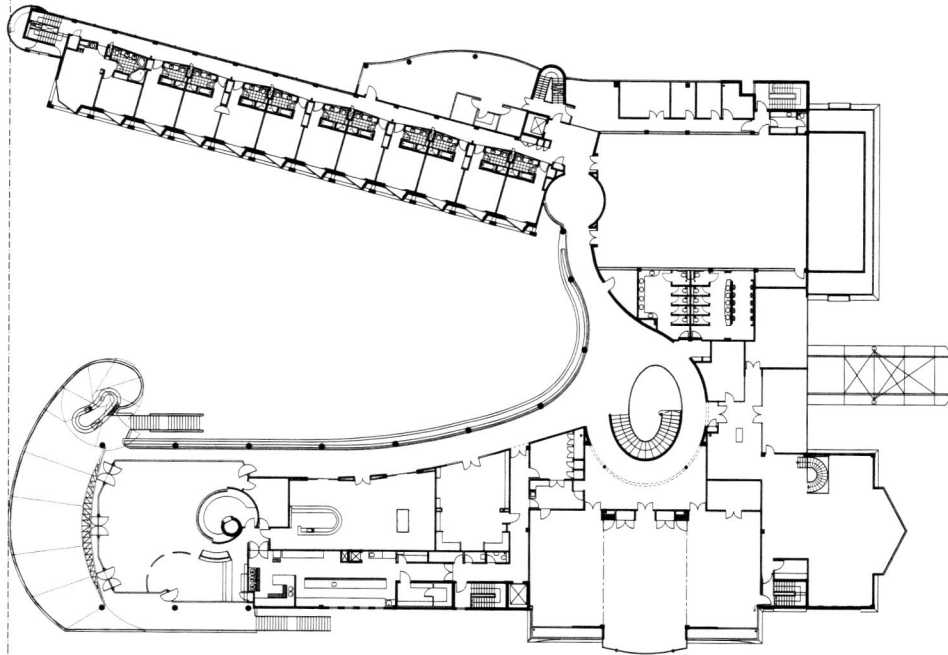

Plan of the second floor.

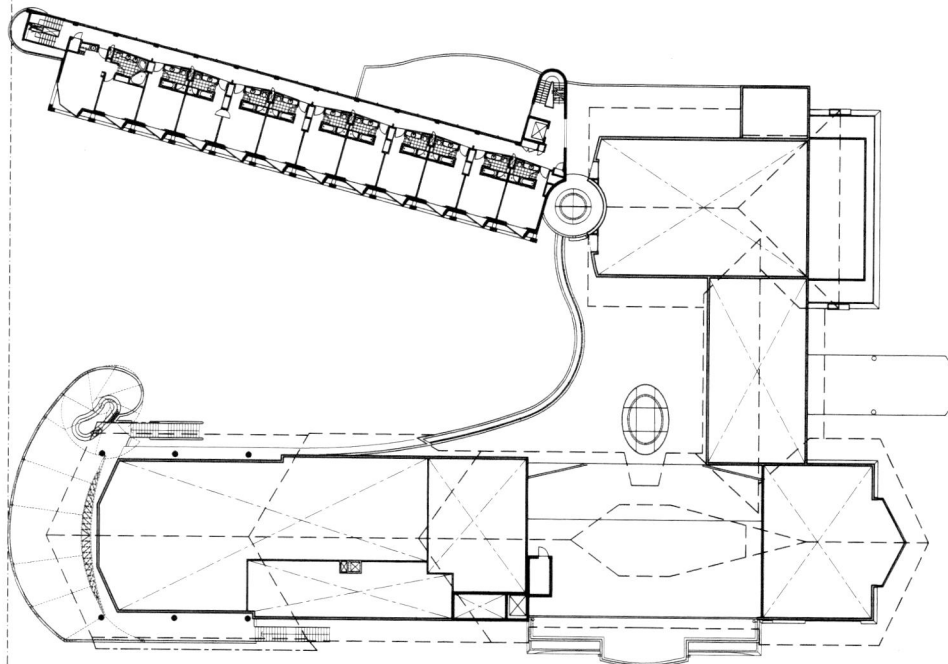

Plan of the first floor.

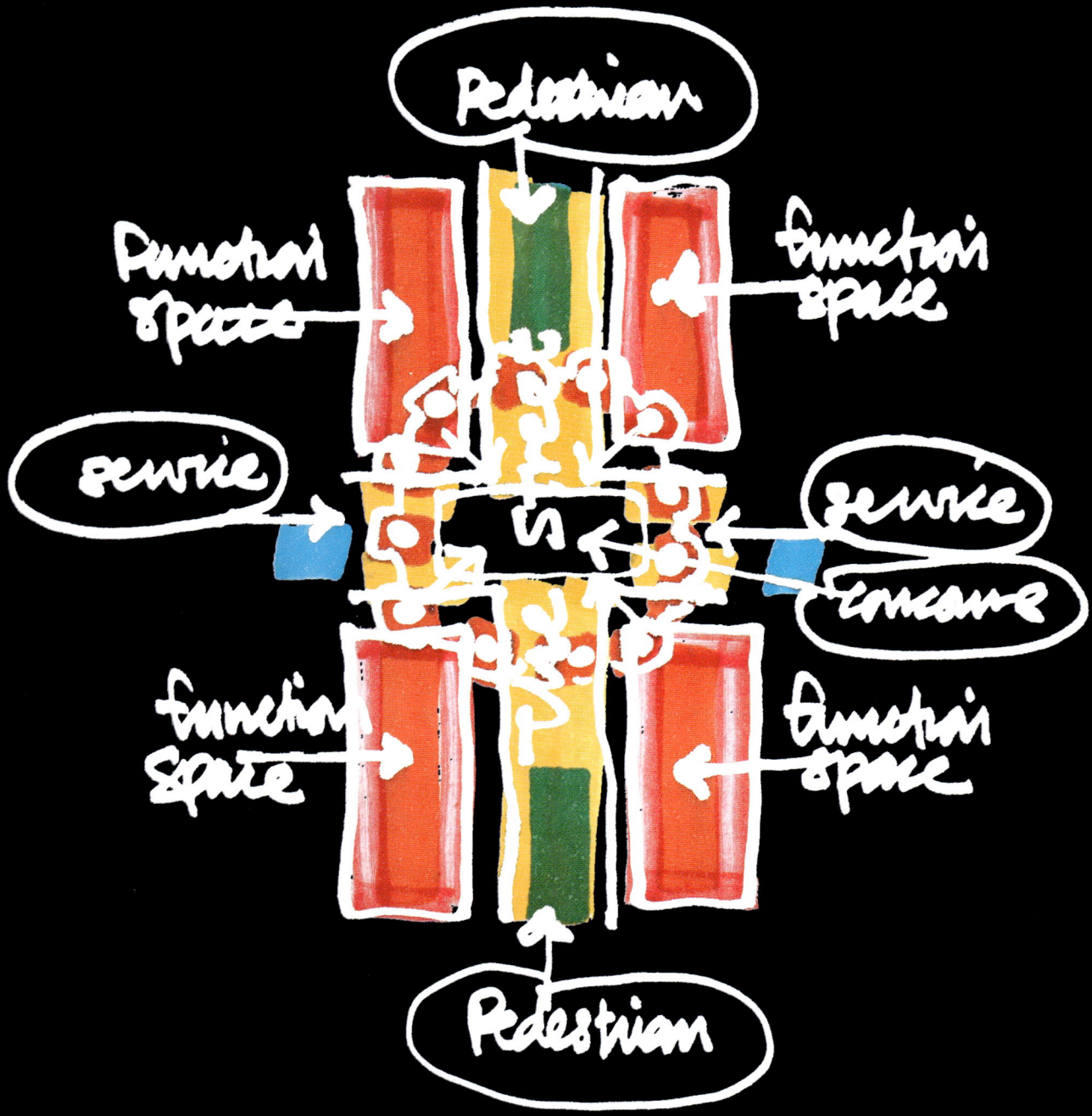

Pedestrian

Function Space

Function Space

service

service

entrance

function Space

function Space

Pedestrian

The Nordic Center
Singapore, 1999

Opposite page,
concept plan
of inter-crossing axial
representing meeting
points of the
Scandinavian countries.

Below, plan of the
second floor.

The Nordic Center is situated in the International Business Park, Singapore. It is an area designated by the local authority for predominantly Research & Development usage. The Nordic Center is to become a business center for the small and medium enterprise of Scandinavian countries. Besides being an incubation center for companies looking for a platform for further expansion into the region, it will be a place for business and social interaction among the Scandinavian and local community. The emphasis of a meeting place with a sense of identity was a starting point for the design of the center.

There are two phases for the development of the Nordic Center, initially planned on a layout of four wings sitting on a cross axial symbolizing unity and the Nordic flags. The first phase is currently under development and the building is to accommodate approximately 20,000 square meters of offices with conference facilities, auditorium, exhibition spaces and a cafeteria. Together with a forecourt that will double-up as outdoor exhibition space to complete the functional brief of the building.

The first half of Nordic Center is a "U" block with a forecourt opening towards the main avenue of the business park. The exposure set an opportunity for the architecture to express a sense of identity at the frontage. The forecourt is also elevated to further improve its prominent position, it shall be used "artistically" as a showcase of both landscape and sculpture related to the Nordic theme.

One of the challenges for the design is to direct the flow of pedestrian traffic from the vehicular drop-off point to the main entrance of the building. The path is to take one across the forecourt protected from the potential heavy tropical downpours. This is resolved through a carefully detailed covered way designed to look like "metal trees" as integral part of sculptural garden and a porte-cochère with its "nautical" outlook suggesting the traditional Scandinavian spirit of exploration.

The building, standing in contrast to its organic forecourt elements, retains a modernist simplicity. The appearance from the exterior is one of clean, sleek images of a technological expression. Sunshades and low-emissivity glass are introduced to complement with the horizontal expression of the cladding and help in reducing the energy consumption of the building.

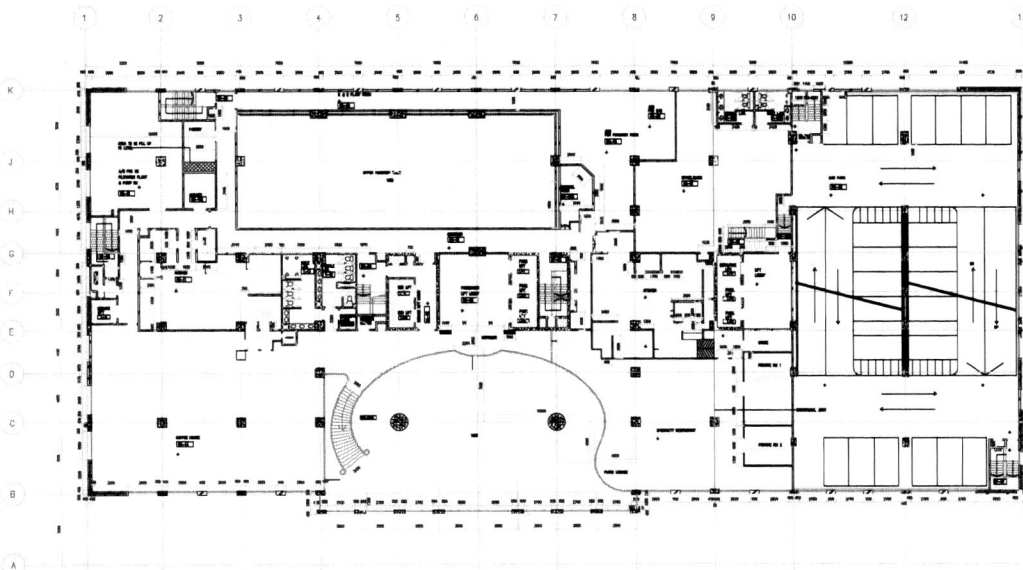

93

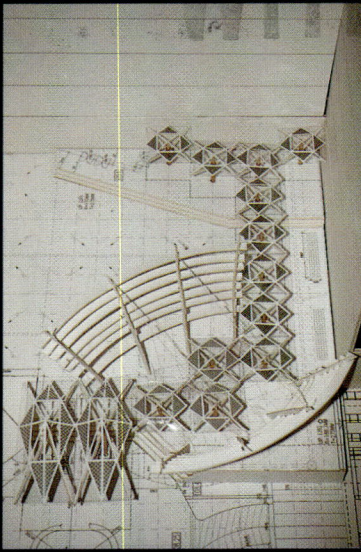

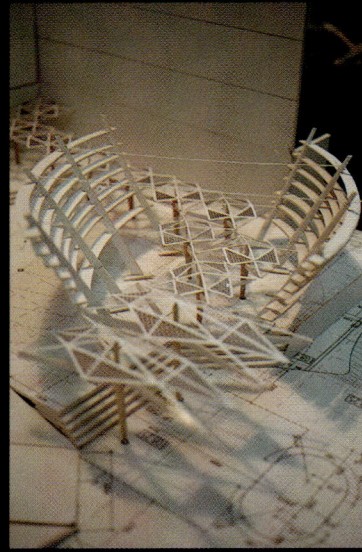

Left and below, study models of the entry forecourt which architectural form derives from a metaphor of a boat.

Opposite page, computer drawing of the proposed Nordic Center showing u-shaped form of building wrapping around the central forecourt and computer perspective highlighting the organic sculpture contrasting against the horizontal modernist elevations behind.

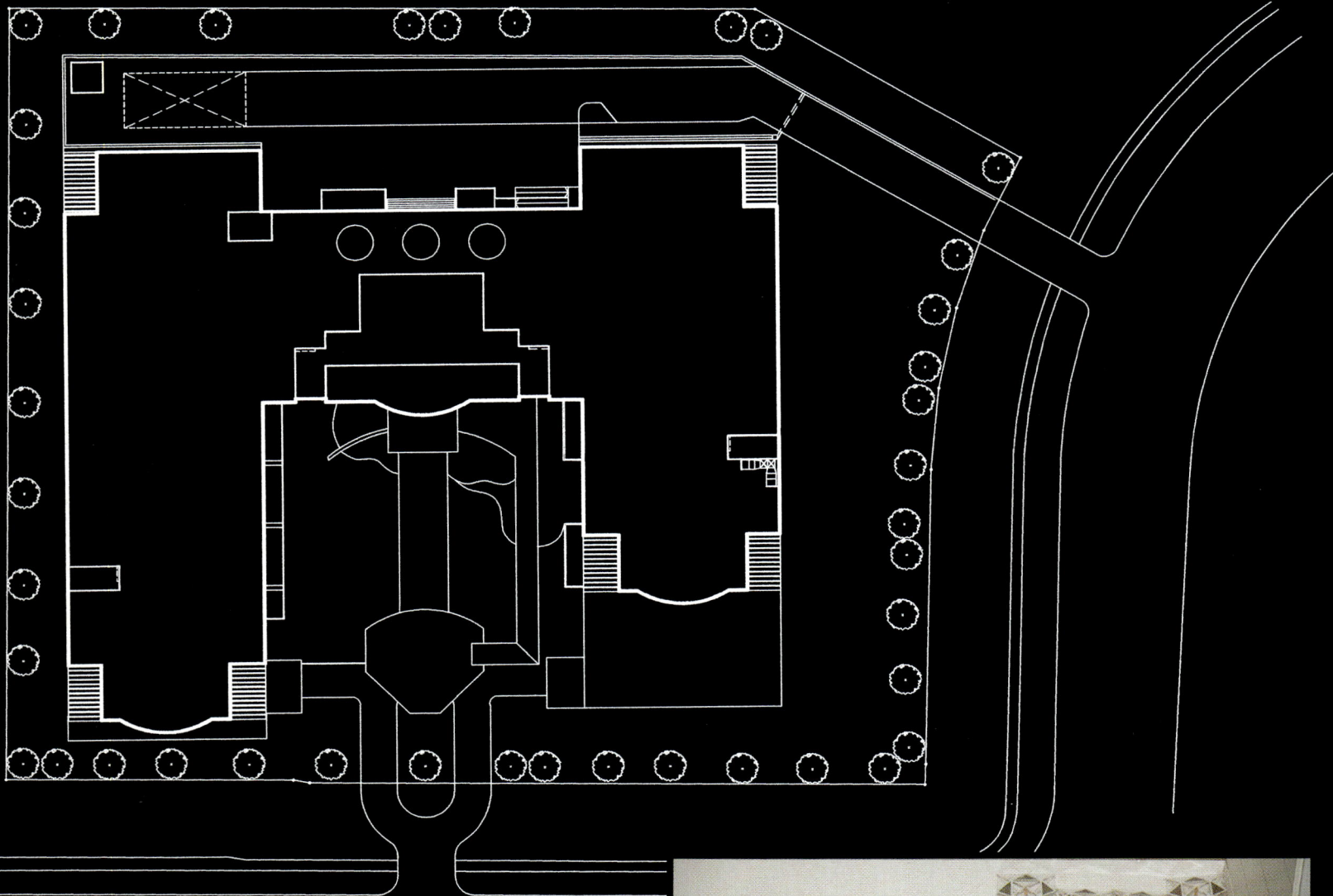

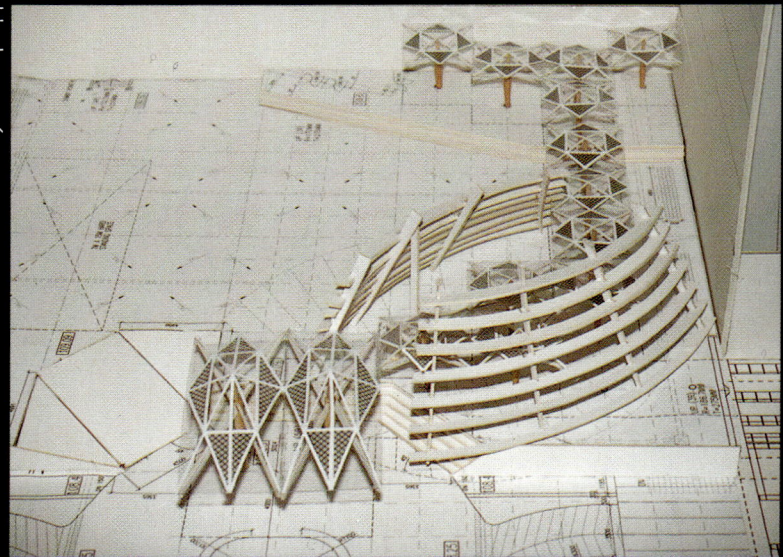

Chinese Chamber of Commerce
Church Street/Telok Ayer Street, Singapore, 1997-2001

WITHDRAWN

Situated in the heart of Singapore's expanding financial district, the proposed China Square concept plan contributes a vibrant, new center of offices, hotels, shops and eateries. The Chinese Chamber of Commerce building, is a proposed development of a 30-storey office building with a four-storey podium, and banking hall at ground level, is located at the "Gateway" to this growth area.

This project has been with us for ten years, and has made its way through many design phases to establish planning principles and embrace additional neighboring lots.

There are, however, consistent aims, over which we have been reluctant to compromise, like achieving a good height of at least 30 storeys, necessary, due to the buildings location on the perimeter of the Central Business Districts (CBD) high-rise zone, with a prominent aspect to western parts of the city. The URA planning parameters demand that we match in the podium height and modulation with those of the neighboring buildings, but we are taking the tower to the ground on the important junction of Telok Ayer and Church Streets, its verticality emphasized with the externally expressed columns.

The new tower will be a light and elegant structure, with sun shaded glass curtain walling creating a distinct and deliberate contrast with the two neighboring commercial developments, which are monolithic towers in granite and glass.

This scheme is now moving into its detail design stages and is currently scheduled for completion early in 2001.

Opposite page, section.

Below, site plan.

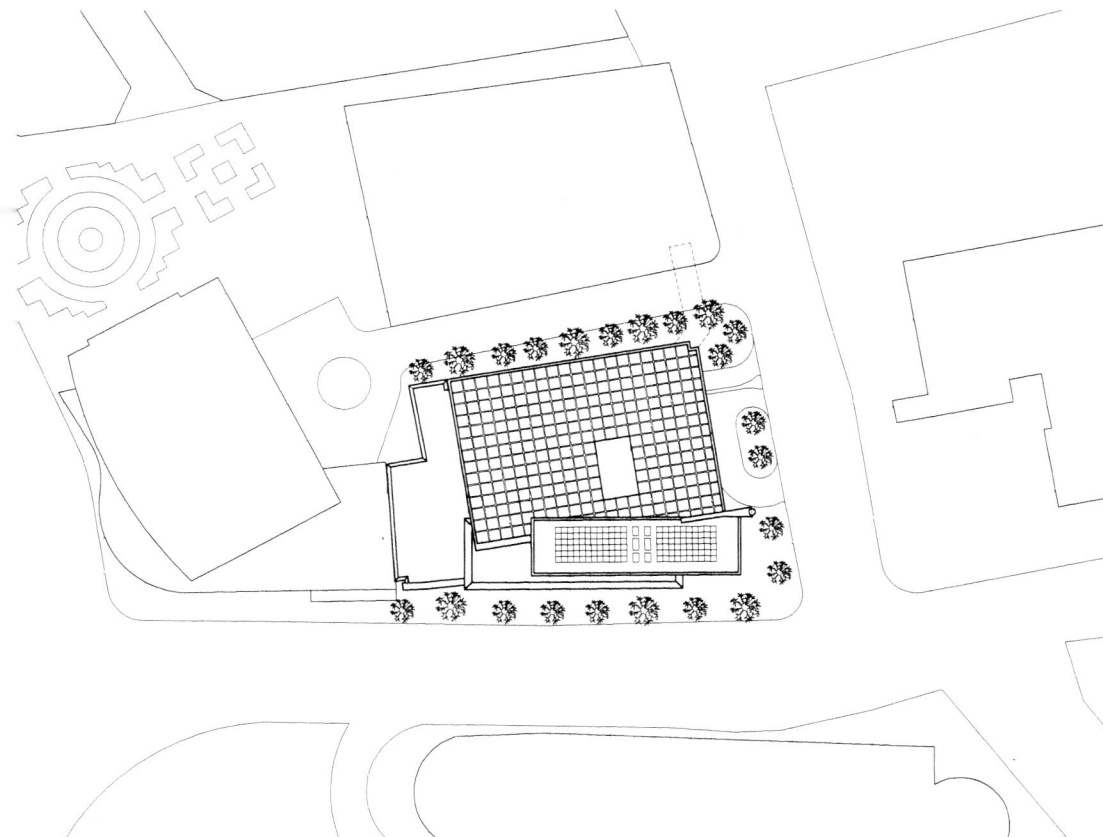

97

Selected Works Data

Marco Polo Hotel
Singapore
Phase 1 Completed in 1968
Number of rooms: 300
Client: Goodwood Park Hotel Singapore
Phase 2 Completed in 1974
Number of rooms: 308
Client: Omni Hotel International

Singapore Polytechnic
Singapore
Completed in 1979
Area: 327,726 sq.m
Built area: 74,320 sq.m

St Joseph's Institution
Malcolm Road, Singapore
Completed in 1987
Completed in 1990
Completed in 1995

Odeon Towers
Singapore
Completed in 1992
No. of storeys: 23
Client: United Overseas Land (UOL)

Raffles Marina
Tuas West Drive Singapore
Completed in 1992
Site Area: 42,374 sq.m
Client: Raffles Natsteel Resorts

Keppel Distripark
for the Port of Singapore Authority
Singapore
Completed in 1993
Area: 137,338 sq.m
Client: Port of Singapore Authority
(PSA)

Singapore Tourist Board
Headquarters, Singapore
Completed in 1995
No. of storeys: 13
Client: Singapore Tourist Promotion Board

Schering Plough Pharmaceutical
Manufacturing Facilities
Tuas West Drive, Singapore
Completed in 1997
Facilities consist of:
Administration Building, 3,200 sq.m
Production Buildings with clean rooms,
10,000 sq.m
Laboratories with clean rooms, 1,800 sq.m
Warehouses, 2,300 sq.m
Boiler House and other auxiliary buildings,
25,000 sq.m
Client: Schering Plough Ltd

The National Museums
Artifacts Repository
(National Heriitage Board)
Jurong Port Road, Singapore
Completed in 1997
Area: 13,600 sq.m
Client: The National Heritage Board of Singapore

Robinson Point
39 Robinson Road, Singapore
Completed in 1997
Number of storeys: 21
Client: DBS Land

Republic of Singapore Yacht Club
Singapore
Currently under construction
Expected date of completion: beginning of 1999
Client: Republic of Singapore Yacht Club

The Nordic Center
Singapore
Expected date of completion: 1999
Area: Approx. 20 000 sq.m

Chinese Chamber of Commerce
Church Street/Telok Ayer Street, Singapore,
Currently in design development stage
No. of storeys: 30
Client: Development Consortium
of Chinese Chamber Realty, Church Street
Prqerties Pte Ltd, and China Square
Holdings Pte Ltd

Biographies

Alfred H K Wong

He was born on 4 January 1930 in Hong Kong. Graduated in 1953 with Honours in Design from Melbourne University. As Managing Director in charge of the firm, his responsibilities lie in the fundamental decision making in regard to policies on design, building quality, and the deployment of key personnel for the various tasks. A constant review of the design quality of all jobs undertained by the office is maintained. His directorship also carries the function of conducting vital interaction between the Singapore office and all the associated firms in London, Sydney, Vienna, Hong Kong, Kuala Lumpur and Penang. In 1957, he founded the firm and since then has worked closely with several ministerial departments, appointed by the Government of Singapore as a Member of the Commission of Enquiry into the Building Industry, sat on the Development Control Committee and was appointed by the Minister of Education as a representative on the Board of Governors for Singapore Polytechnic. From 1963 to 1965 he was the President of the Singapore Institute of Architects and retained a council member position until 1972 before becoming a member of the Institute's Practise Committee. That same year his affiliation with the country's leading university began with his position as the SIA representative on the Council of University of Singapore. Over the next decade, his numerous appointments included positions with the Energy Conservation Building Committee (set up by the Public Works Department), the Public Service Disciplinary Panel, the Ministry of the Architectural Design Panel, the Mass Rapid Transit Authority, and the URA Restoration and Development Panel for Raffles Hotel, Bugis Junction and Albert Court. His capacity as a human dynamo continues into the nineties. From 1990, he was appointed member of the Architectural Design Panel by the Minister for National Development, Director of Technology Parks Pte. Ltd., Committee member of Jurong Town Corporation Advisory on Research and Development, and Member of the CHIJ Supervisory Panel for the URA. His current portfolio includes a position on the Design and Aesthetics Advisory Group of Singapore's Arts Centre. He was the President of the Rotary Club of Singapore from 1996 to 1997.

Edward H Y Wong

He was born on 21 June 1936 in Hong Kong. Graduated in 1961 as a Bachelor of Architecture with Honours from Liverpool University. As a Senior Partner in charge of the firm, his responsibilities lie in the direct role of Director in charge of design and documentation on many different major projects including masterplanning, residential, and retail and commercial complexes. His particular area of expertise, however, lies in marina design in which he is a leading consultant as a result of his experience as a keen ocean-going yachtsman. His professional record as an active member of the Singapore Institute of Architects began in 1965 when he became a member of the Publication Committee. In the following two years he was a Council Member and held a position on the Practice Committee. In 1968, he became Honorary Secretary of the Singapore Planning and Urban Research Group, later promoted to Chairman until 1970. The same year, he was appointed by the Minister for Law and National Development as alternative representative of the Singapore Institute of Architects on the Development Control Committee, and a Member of the Singapore Planning and Urban Research Group. In 1983 his involvements extended to connect with the University and was appointed as an external examiner for the University of Singapore, and later continued his affiliation with the SIA as a Council Member and Chairman of the Practise Committee. In 1988 he was made Honorary Secretary and two years later became the Vice-President.

Ang Choon Kiat

He was born on 10 May 1943 in Johor, Malaysia. Graduated with a diploma in Architecture from Singapore Polytechnic in 1969. As a Director of the Company, his role as Director in charge of projects includes regular responsibilities but also extends to recognise his expertise in CAD and graphics.

He set up the computerisation of the firm. His specialist area in architecture is industrial buildings and his portfolio includes projects for Rhone-Poulenc, Schering Plough, Fisons, Firmenich, and the German Centre for Industry and Trade, amongst educational and institutional buildings. His professional record includes a long association with the Singapore Institute of Architects as a Council Member. Other involvements extend to the area of community service as a member of The National Council of Social Services' House and Building Committee, The Singapore Children Society Convalescent Home Committee, and Volunteer Service to the Movement of Intellectually Disabled.

Goh Peng Thong

He was born on 26 April 1947 in Malaysia. Graduated in 1973 as a Bachelor of Architecture from the University of Singapore. As a Company Director, his responsibilities lie as the Director in charge of varying projects ranging from health care facilities, hotel/commercial, and residential development. His specialist area however, focuses on hotel development and projects to his credit include the Marco Polo Hotel extension, Ming Court Hotel in Kuala Lumpur and Holiday Inn Crowne Plaza in Xiamen, PRC.

For a number of years his association with the Singapore Institute of Architects as a representative for various Government Departments involving the process of Governmental approvals for building projects, has kept the current requirements of the Government constantly in view. During the eighties he held active positions on numerous boards and committees. These included Chairman of the SISIR Technical Committee, Council Member of the SIA, Member of the Practise Committee, and later a panel member on the Investigation Committee of the Board of Architects. In 1982 he was a Committee Member of Energy Conservation and a Member of the Singapore Building Construction Safety and Health Advisory Committee. His knowledge of building codes extended to the appointment of the position of Chairman of Regulations, Codes and Standards Committee and Member of Standing Committee of the Fire Safety Bureau, and Representative for the SIA on Plot Ratio calculation. In 1990, he was Chairman of Examiners for Professional Practice Examinations and continues to maintain an active role in that area.